FEDAYEEN

FEDAYEEN

Guerrillas Against Israel

by
ZEEV SCHIFF
and
RAPHAEL ROTHSTEIN

David McKay Company, Inc.
New York

FEDAYEEN

LIBRARY OF CONGRESS CATALOG CARD NUMBER: 72-188270
MANUFACTURED IN THE UNITED STATES OF AMERICA

Acknowledgments

The authors are grateful for assistance received from representatives of the following organizations: American-Israel Public Affairs Committee; American Jewish Committee; Arab Information Center, New York; B'nai B'rith Anti-Defamation League; Ha'aretz; Israeli Army informa-officers; the library of Israel Defense Forces Headquarters; Organization of Arab Students; New York Times News Service; Palestine Liberation Organization; and the Shiloach Institute, Tel Aviv.

A special debt is owed to Ron Cohen, Y. Harkabi, Kennett L. Rawson and F. J. & H. Spieler for their counsel, kindness, and cooperation.

Contents

FEDAYEEN

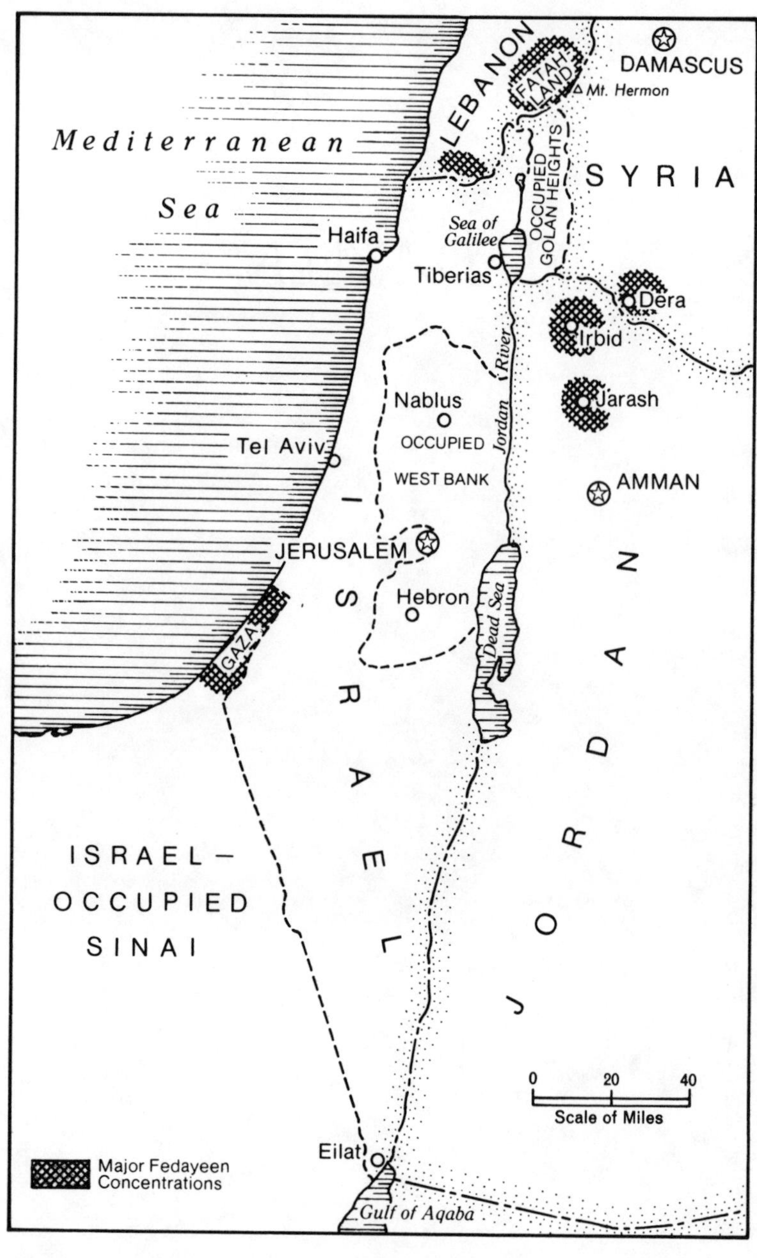

Mediterranean
Sea
LEBANON
FATAH-LAND
DAMASCUS
Mt. Hermon
SYRIA
OCCUPIED GOLAN HEIGHTS
Sea of Galilee
Haifa
Tiberias
Dera
Irbid
Jordan River
Jarash
Nablus
OCCUPIED
WEST BANK
Tel Aviv
AMMAN
ISRAEL
JERUSALEM
Hebron
Dead Sea
GAZA
JORDAN
ISRAEL—
OCCUPIED
SINAI
0
20
40
Scale of Miles
Eilat
Major Fedayeen Concentrations
Gulf of Aqaba

CHAPTER 1

The Palestinian Consciousness

Any approach to the Arab-Israeli conflict must consider the sufferings and aspirations of the Palestinians. Since the displacement of the Palestinian Arabs and their dispersion throughout the Arab and Western world over twenty years ago as a result of the Arab rejection of a United Nations plan to partition Palestine into Jewish and Arab states, the concept of Palestinian nationhood has grown in strength and influence.

Wherever one encounters Palestinians, whether in the squalid refugee camps of Jordan and Lebanon or in the cities of the Arab world, they express a common aspiration to return to their homes in what is now Israel.

The historical process that has led to the present national consciousness of the Palestinians is fraught with claims and counterclaims, bitterness, and sad ironies. It is a confused story of two peoples with equal justice in conflict over the same land. While it is true that Jewish settlement in Palestine has been achieved to some degree at the expense of the indigenous Arab population, it is no less demonstrable that the stubborn, willful, and self-destructive refusal of the Arabs to recognize and accommodate Jewish national claims has been a basic cause of the violence and tension in this seeming irreconcilable dispute.

Those who reject the validity of the Palestinian claim to nationhood correctly point out that there never was a nation known as Palestine and that most of those who fled the section of Palestine granted by the United Nations to Israel had lived in the land for less than a generation. Indeed, much of the land in dispute had never belonged to individual Arabs but to rich Arab landowners who, more often than not, spent most of their time in comfort in Paris, Beirut, or Cairo while Palestinian peasants worked their land as sharecroppers. Furthermore, a good deal of the land the Jews had settled had been purchased from Turkish and Arab landowners from 1880 to 1948 by the Jewish National Fund.

Under the British Mandate there was hardly any consciousness of a distinct Palestinian entity. The few hundred thousand Arabs living in the Turkish province known as Palestine at the time of the Balfour Declaration[1] and the British occupation in 1917 did not think of themselves as Palestinians. Most peasants thought of themselves as southern Syrians and political life was dominated by two rival factions owing allegiance to Syrian nationalists or the Hashemite rulers.

As Jewish immigration increased over the years there

were sporadic manifestations of violent opposition on the part of the Arabs, but it was not until the Arab rebellion of 1936 that Palestinian nationalism was finally recognized as a force unalterably opposed to the British Mandate and Jewish settlement. The 1936 uprising led to the British White Paper of 1939 that limited Jewish immigration, but this success was dissipated by the leaders who allowed the British, assisted by the Hashemites, to Arabize the Palestinian problem and to involve and confuse Palestinian nationalism with the struggle of other Arab nations to throw off colonial rule. The leadership of the Palestinians was assumed by families and men who looked to either the British or the Egyptians, the Hashemites, or Saudis for their support. The advent of World War II served to further fragment Middle Eastern politics and the cause of Palestine became secondary. It was thus that when the violent disturbances that followed the United Nations vote on partition erupted, the men who had dominated Palestinian politics took refuge in neighboring Arab lands and were absent when the Arab armies invaded. Against this background of fear and confusion the leaderless and bewildered Arab communities of Haifa, Jaffa, Lydda, and Jerusalem fled in large numbers from Palestine.

From 1948 to 1967 the world heard little about the Palestinian entity. The late emergence of Palestinian nationalism is indicated by the fact that those Arabs who remained on the western bank of the Jordan River after the 1948 war did not set up a Palestinian state. Instead, the land was annexed by King Abdullah of Jordan in 1949 and the almost 500,000 Arabs living there became Jordanian citizens.

The majority of the estimated 600,000 to 700,000 Arabs who fled Palestine between 1947 and 1948 were settled in refugee camps in Jordan, Syria, Lebanon, and the Gaza Strip, then under Egyptian control. Only in Jordan were the Palestinians granted citizenship and offered some opportunity of integration since the country was so small. Those Palestinians who had fled with their fortunes intact or who had money abroad were able to settle into new lives with a minimum of difficulty. In Beirut, Saudi Arabia, Kuwait, and the oil sheikdoms of the Persian Gulf, educated, ambitious Palestinians distinguished themselves in many fields and new fortunes were made. But the bulk of these displaced people existed as refugees, supported by United Nations funds and utilized as pawns in the constant game of nations played in the Arab world. Today 1.4 million Palestinian refugees are listed on United Nations Relief and Works Agency rolls but many of the names are fictitious, belonging to dead or nonexistent persons.

In the squalor and enforced idleness of the camps, Palestine was seen as the nation the refugees had lost. They were strangers in the other Arab countries and despite ties of language and religion (Islam and Christianity) even those Palestinians not confined to camps but able to move about freely found it difficult to assimilate. A strong sense of common identity was preserved and attachment to Palestine persisted despite the passage of time, hardships, and exile. Children born in the UNRWA camps who had never seen Palestine said when asked: "I am from Haifa" or "I am from Jaffa."

The Palestinian exile was exploited by the Arab nations for tactical and political reasons. At Arab League meetings in the early 1960s the idea of the Palestinian entity and the call for Palestinians to assume the key role in the struggle against Israel were aired by various leaders with little concern for the plight of the refugees.

But for the Palestinians themselves these ideas were

the substance of a consciousness that had at its core the notion of return. Running against the ideological tide of pan-Arab unity as preached by the late Gamal Abdel Nasser and other Arab powers, the Palestinians saw themselves as a distinct group. This feeling was nurtured by common suffering, the difficulty of absorption into Arab countries, and living en masse in refugee camps. Ironically, the Zionist example may have served to inspire the rising sense of nationhood. The Jews had preserved a strong attachment to the land of Israel for 2000 years of dispersion and exile. The Palestinians bitterly concluded that they could do no less. One Arab writer noted in the early 1960s that a "new Zionism" was formed among the refugees.[2]

The education young Palestinians received in the camps indoctrinated them with an ideology of return. They were taught that a tragic wrong was inflicted on the Palestinians and that justice required that Israel be liquidated. At home these youths, who constitute the majority of the Palestinian refugees today, were told stories of their parents' former houses. As is natural with deprived people, memory became a form of escape and with the passage of time modest houses became mansions and small holdings took on the dimensions of vast estates. The ideological attachment of the youth was no less intense than the actual link of their parents.

In Arab writings the sense of longing for return to the lost land of Palestine was often expressed in vivid and emotional terms. An oft-quoted example is a passage in Nasir Al-Din Al-Nashashibi's book, *Return Ticket*, (Beirut, 1962):

> Every year I shall say to my little son: "We shall return my son, and you will be with me; we shall return; we shall return to our land and walk there

barefoot. We'll remove our shoes so that we may feel the holiness of the ground beneath us. We'll blend our souls with its air and earth. We'll walk till we come to the orange trees; we'll feel the sand and water; we'll kiss seed and fruit; we'll sleep in the shade of the first tree we meet; we'll pay homage to the first martyr's grave we come across. We'll turn here and there to trace our lives. Where are they? Here with this village square, with this mosque's minaret, with the beloved field, the desolate wall, with the remains of a tottering fence, and a building whose traces have been erased. Here are our lives. Each grain of sand teaches us about our life. Do you not remember Jaffa and its delightful shore, Haifa and its lofty mountain, Bet Shean and the fields of crops and fruit, Nazareth and the Christians' bells, Acre and the memories of al-Jazzar, Ibrahim Pasha, Napoleon and the fortress, the streets of Jerusalem, my dear Jerusalem, Tiberias and its peaceful shore with the golden waves, Majdal and the remnant of my kin in its land?"

This lyrical and touching expression of love for the country is offset by violent hatred toward the Israelis on the page following the above passage. In it the author describes the effect his earlier words will have on his son:

> I shall see the hatred in the eyes of my son and your sons. I shall see how they take revenge. If they do not know how to take revenge, I shall teach them. And if they agree to a truce or peace, I shall fight against them as I fight against my enemy and theirs. I want them to be callous, to be ruthless, to take revenge. I want them to wash away the disaster of

> 1948 with the blood of those who prevent them from entering their land. Their homeland is dear to them, but revenge is dearer. We'll enter their lairs in Tel Aviv. We'll smash Tel Aviv with axes, guns, hands, fingernails, and teeth, while singing the songs of Kibiy a Dir Yasin and Nasir ad-Din.[3] We shall sing the hymns of the triumphant, avenging return . . .

Recognition of the Palestinian Arabs' deep connection to the land is not unusual among Israelis, many of whom favor some form of accommodation with the Palestinians. The basic dilemma of the Palestine problem is that while a certain responsiveness to the Palestinian aspiration has been noted on the part of many Israelis, no responsible or representative Palestinian leader has shown any willingness to temper the quest for annihilation of Israel. This fundamental conflict of desires thwarts the possibility of enduring peace in the Middle East, but at the same time allows the Palestinian nationhood movement to feed on pristine forms of resentment and hatred.

Palestinian intellectuals and professional men who formed a kind of leadership in the years following 1948 made special efforts to instill the Palestinian attachment among the less fortunate refugees. A process of creating a people without territory through education, history, folklore, and other means was carried on by the upper-class Palestinians who themselves were able to find work and a place in the economic and social life of the Arab nations. The refugees were not unmindful of the disparity between their miserable lives in the camps and the comfortable bourgeois existence of their mentors. For this reason, the Palestinian leadership, such as it was, was regarded with cynicism and distrust.

The refugees were also ambivalent in their relations

with the Arab states. Complaints against the Arab countries were that they had not fulfilled their obligations to the Palestinians, had manipulated them and used their problem as a strategem in their own rivalries while showing indifference to the refugees' suffering. But there were also feelings of gratitude toward the Arab nations, for despite the difficulties of absorption some could find work and their children could study in these countries. The Palestinians also realized that in the war against Israel they were dependent on the military support of the Arab states.

A certain inconsistency and confusion is also noted in the way the conflict with Israel has been envisioned. Until 1948 the conflict was essentially between Israel and the Palestinians. Then the intervention of the Arab states and the ensuing war with Israel diminished the role of the Palestinians. It was not until the early 1960s that the Palestinians were again to gain a prominence that would be enhanced by the experience of the Six-Day War. Throughout these years of shifting emphasis and changing external political conditions two significant developments among the Palestinians were taking place—a cohesiveness and sense of common destiny was growing and their concept of warfare with Israel was being radicalized. A younger, leftist-minded generation preaching a new activism had begun challenging the traditional leadership. These younger men of varying backgrounds and experience were influenced by the ideas of Mao Tse-tung, the Algerian FLN, and the Cuban revolution. They thought in terms of guerrilla struggle and national liberation. Guerrilla organizations known as *Fedayeen* came into being and formulated Marxist ideologies and theories about a revolutionary Palestinian state. Israel was seen as the "running dog" of Western imperialism in the Middle East. The demise of the Arab armies in the Six-Day War led to an elevation of the status of the fedayeen who emerged as the standard bearers of Arab nationalism and pride. Thus, from a marginal role in the post-1948 years, the Palestinians once again became the main protagonists against Israel, the avant-garde of the Arab struggle. The liberation of Palestine became the chief Arab shibboleth.

When speaking of the Palestinians the reference is actually to two main groups: the first consists of close to 400,000 residents in the densely populated Gaza Strip, including approximately 210,000 refugees in UNRWA camps, and the 500,000 Palestinians—including 60,000 refugees—on the West Bank of the Jordan River, which is now occupied by Israel as a result of the Six-Day War. The West Bank comprises two regions called Judea and Samaria and Arabs who were living on the West Bank before 1948 and also those who fled at the time of the first Arab-Israeli war live there now.

The second Palestinian group is made up of refugees in camps and permanent residents living outside territory under Israeli control. These Palestinians number about a million and live in camps in Jordan, Lebanon, and Syria as well as in the cities of the Arab Middle East. The majority, some 700,000, live in Jordan and account for almost half of that country's population. Another 300,000 are divided about equally between Lebanon and Syria. In the absence of reliable figures[4] it is difficult to determine the total number of Palestinians today—Arabs who were born in the area of the former British mandate and their offspring—but it is probably around 2 million.

The West Bank and Gaza Strip Palestinians are perforce in daily contact with the Israeli authorities. Any move they might make toward regularizing their situation, such as the establishment of an autonomous West

Bank Palestinian state, is viewed with suspicion and hostility by other Palestinians, particularly the fedayeen who have terrorized them, and the surrounding Arab states. For this reason, as well as the cautious leadership on the West Bank and in Gaza, and Israel's hesitancy no progress toward a settlement with Israel or change in their status has been achieved in the four years since the Six-Day War.

Many in this group live in fear of a renewed Arab-Israeli war since they are liable to be principal victims. A settlement that might prevent another war would be directly in their interest. But the bonds of kinship, and feeling of national pride as well as the uncertain status of the occupied territories make it difficult for these Palestinians to act independently of outside Arab considerations and the fedayeen's passionate demands for repatriation and dominion over the entire area—the West Bank and Israel proper as defined by the pre-June, 1967 cease-fire lines.

The second group of Palestinians living away from Israeli occupation has responded to the growing radicalization of the Arab world by supporting the fedayeen movement whose leaders come from the university-educated and professional segment. They vehemently oppose any political settlement, regardless of frontiers or conditions because their opposition is to the principle of a Jewish state in any form whatsoever. The present decline of the fedayeen as a result of King Hussein's relentless drive against them in Jordan cannot be expected to alter the unrealistic, but nonetheless fervent, goal of banishing two and a half million Jews from Israel and establishing a Palestinian nation in its place. This goal is the essential element in the unifying consciousness of the Palestinians.

Although their destinies once were controlled and manipulated by one or another Arab state, the Palestinians today are no longer pawns in the internecine struggle of the Arab nations. They themselves, however, are not immune to ideological differences and internal squabbling as evidenced by the feuding among the various fedayeen groups. Despite this factionalism there is a new sense of definition and commitment animating them. It is now obvious, or should be, that no matter what prolonged and intricate negotiations Egypt, Israel, the United States, and the Soviet Union conduct there will be no peace in the Middle East unless the Palestinian aspiration to national existence is in some way satisfied.

Self-awareness has come late to the Palestinians, but it has developed rapidly. In the short time that has elapsed since the June 1967 war the word "Palestine" is important in the world's vocabulary. The first significant expression of the new Palestinian nationalism has been the fedayeen and the Palestine Liberation movement.

The fedayeen were the first among the Arabs to show signs of revival in the atmosphere of despair and futility that followed the Six-Day War. While the Arab armies were still nursing their wounds, Fatah came forth with plans to renew the conflict with Israel. No longer was there talk of an all-out offensive; now the term "people's war" began to be heard and the concept of the "Palestinian revolt" introduced as the motive for a campaign of terror.

On June 20, 1967, less than two weeks after the Six-Day War, Fatah headquarters, after a heated debate, issued the following announcement: "Our organization has decided to continue struggling against the Zionist conquerer. However, we are planning to operate far from the Arab states so they won't have to suffer Israeli reprisals for fedayeen actions. It will therefore be impossible to hold the Arab people responsible for our war. Our organization is the organization of the Palestinian people and we are united in our resolve to free our stolen homeland from the hands of the Zionists."

The leaders of Fatah were convinced that the conditions were right for a Palestinian people's war against Israel. They saw the postwar situation as one in which an internal guerrilla struggle could develop in the Arab territories now occupied by Israel. Overnight Israel had assumed control over a large population of Palestinian Arabs. Suddenly added to Israel's three million population (including 333,000 Israeli Arabs) were the almost one million Arabs living in the West Bank and the Gaza Strip.

"Israel has swallowed a serpent," some Palestinian leaders claimed. The reference was to one million men, women, and children who had been exposed for years to virulent anti-Jewish propaganda and were politically aware and interested in proving themselves as an entity distinct from Jordan—a Palestinian entity.

The vast new areas under Israel's control—an increase from 12,000 square miles before the Six-Day War to 54,000 square miles, including the Sinai peninsula's 37,000 square miles—also suggested enormous possibilities for guerrilla warfare. Now mountainous areas offered the fedayeen hidden terrain for bases.

Political circumstances also appeared to be working against Israel because of her insistence on direct talks with the Arabs and a genuine peace settlement as conditions for her withdrawal from the occupied territories. A shift of sympathy to the Arab "underdogs" was noticeable in leftist circles and both the Communist bloc and traditional anti-Semites were able to exploit the realignment of commitments to operate against Israel politically and diplomatically.

Israel was cast as the "conquerer," expansionist and

aggressive. The image of a strong, self-reliant Jewish nation was more than many influential elements of the Christian world could accept. In the past, sympathy for the Jews was based on their plight as helpless victims whose existence was threatened. At the United Nations and other international forums a strong anti-Israel bias emerged. Jerusalem was regarded as unreasonable and stubborn to insist that the humiliated Arabs negotiate a peace directly. Israel was called on to consider Arab sensibilities. These new currents of thinking were not lost on the Palestinian extremists. The world's memory is short and soon the peril that faced Israel in May, 1967, was forgotten. By projecting themselves as national liberation fighters, rather than merely saboteurs and terrorists, the fedayeen groups elicited sympathy from the international Left, which equated defeat with virtue, and was therefore ready to abandon defense of Israel's national rights and take up the Palestinian cause.

The dangers the new territorial and political situation presented to Israel were commented on by Defense Minister Moshe Dayan in October, 1967:

> I don't think this talk about Arab guerrilla warfare on the model of the Vietcong is serious. I'm confident that we'll succeed in coping with Arab terrorism if we behave correctly. This, in large part, means not to desire to rule over every aspect of life in the administered territories. A guerrilla war is essentially a struggle between the conquered and the conquerers. As long as the guerrilla struggle is between a conquered people and a foreign invader it has a chance of succeeding. But here the situation is basically different unless, of course, we assume the role of conquerer. When guerrilla war is not waged be-

tween conquered and the conquerer, but between two nations or communities it cannot achieve its final aim and often fails altogether. By behaving correctly and not striving to control the lives of all the individuals in the territories or attempting with 2.5 million Jews to rule over a million and a quarter Arabs linked to the Arab countries we will be moving in the right direction.

NOTES

1. The statement issued by the British Government declaring sympathy with "Jewish Zionist aspirations" that put Britain on record as favoring the establishment of a Jewish national home.
2. A. L. Tibawi, "Visions of the Return; The Palestine Refugees in Arabic Poetry and Art," *The Middle East Journal, 17*, (1963), pp. 507–526.
3. Villages frequently mentioned in Arabic writing as examples of Jewish terrorism.
4. No proper refugee census has ever been carried out and these figures are based on various sources, including United Nations, Israeli, and private statistics.

CHAPTER 2

The Time of the Fedayeen

On the night of January 2, 1965, a small group of men entered a hut near the Jordanian border village of Shuna. Three members of the group were dressed in khaki and carried weapons. A short, balding man took charge and gave the others final instructions on the basis of an old map.

The three in combat dress then left the hut and crossed the Jordan River into Israel from a point south of the Sea of Galilee. Since Israeli border surveillance was rather sporadic at this time, there was little chance that the infiltrators would encounter a patrol.

They made their way westward, further into Israeli

territory, and at a pre-determined point turned north. Their instructions were to blow up the Ilbon pumping station, part of Israel's $40 million National Water Carrier, which brought water for irrigation from the Jordan River and Sea of Galilee in the north to the sandy reaches of the Negev, Israel's arid desert to the south.

Along the way the would-be saboteurs must have decided that their mission was too difficult and dangerous. The pumping station was heavily guarded by Israeli border patrols and Druze watchmen. Instead of attempting to blow up the installation, the three threw their explosives into an open channel, hoping that they would flow into a nearby tunnel and explode there. But the saboteurs bungled the job. Because of a malfunctioning timing mechanism the charge was not detonated.

The next day one of the Israeli watchmen spotted a brown sack with Arabic markings floating in one of the canals near the pumping station. Investigation of the package revealed a quantity of explosives attached to a timing mechanism consisting of a large Japanese-made alarm clock. Police scouts retraced the path of the saboteurs and discovered they had crossed back into Jordan and disappeared.

Acting on orders from the military censor, the Israeli press did not report the incident at the time. The saboteurs' identity was a mystery. Several Arab villages were in the area where the incident took place, but there was nothing to link the unsuccessful sabotage attempt with local Arabs. What no one in Israel realized was that by means of this abortive mission a Palestinian fedayeen group calling itself Fatah had launched a wave of terrorist actions against the Jewish state.

January, 1965 marked the beginning of Fatah's active period and the first stage of a chain of events and reactions that would once again inflame the Arab-Israeli conflict, precipitate the Six-Day War and, after a decline of eighteen years, make the Palestinians a force to be reckoned with in the Arab world.

Fatah's first mission was characteristic of later endeavors. The sack of explosives carried by the three men in the beginning of January bore a Jordanian address, and it was clear that Fatah intended the blame to be placed on the Hashemite Kingdom of King Hussein—Jordan. The center of Fatah's activities in the early days was Lebanon and Syria, but in order to mislead Israel and compromise Hussein, Jordan was chosen as the base for launching raids on Israel.

The choice of an irrigation project, an essentially civilian installation, was also indicative of fedayeen thinking. Aiming a blow at the National Water Carrier was motivated by both strategic and psychological reasons. The ambitious hydraulic engineering feat stood as a symbol of Arab impotence in the face of Israeli determination. For years the Arab-League nations had threatened never to allow Israel to divert part of the Jordan River to create a system of national irrigation. The Arab threats had proved empty and by choosing the pumping station for their first target, Fatah hoped not only to hurt Israel but to provoke those Arab nations the Palestinians believed were not defending Arab rights into a renewed conflict.

A few days after the first Fatah attempt, an Israeli Army patrol encountered five infiltrators in a rural region south of Jerusalem. In an exchange of fire, two Israelis were wounded and one seriously injured Arab was left behind by his comrades who fled the scene. After treatment in an Israeli hospital, the abandoned fedayeen, Mahmoud Hijazi, a Jordanian citizen, was interrogated. Hijazi said he was born in Jerusalem and following the partition in 1948 had gone to live in Aqaba, Jordan's Red Sea port. He told his questioners that from 1956 to 1957 he had served in the Jordanian National Guard and afterward was transferred to the Hussein Ben Ali Brigade of the Jordanian Army. He was soon discharged for "criminal activities" and also revealed that some years earlier he had been sentenced to a home for delinquent youth for several unspecified crimes.

Hijazi described meeting a man who persuaded him to join Fatah and promised him good pay for carrying out sabotage in Israel. Together with four other residents of Jordan, Hijazi crossed the Israeli border with the intention of blowing up a pumping station but was surprised by the Israeli patrol. His capture marked the first time a member of a new terrorist organization with the then unfamiliar name of Fatah had fallen into Israeli hands.

In the ensuing weeks a pattern of attempted sabotage raids on Israeli border settlements and irrigation installations was noticed. Israeli intelligence files reveal that the name "Fatah" first appeared at the end of the 1950s in connection with a Lebanese periodical. Nothing more was known about the group except for an announcement broadcast by Radio Cairo on January 13, 1965:

> This is an announcement of Fatah. A force from the first unit of the Third Company attacked the Jordan River diversion installation and succeeded in damaging installations in the Ilbon station's tunnel and the Bet Netofa valley.

The same message appeared in leaflets circulated the day of the broadcast in Beirut and Damascus. Soon Syria began broadcasting accounts of the widespread operations of the Arab "storm troopers" in the heart of occupied Palestine. The alleged attack on the pumping station and other actions were cited and the "bewilderment" of the Israelis was emphasized.

Now Fatah was emerging from anonymity to exposure through uninhibited propaganda. Fatah was described as a political group with a military arm called "Al Atzifa" (The Storm). For the first time, Fatah's hymn was published. In the song the names of Arab terrorist leaders killed in the 1948 Arab-Israeli war and the sites of several battles are commemorated.

The first inflated accounts of Fatah's operations raised the question why this organization came into being precisely in 1965, a relatively tranquil period in Arab-Israeli relations. For several years, the borders had been quiet, and the attack on Israeli-border settlements by Egyptian mercenaries that had years earlier introduced the term "fedayeen" to the world press had been halted by the Sinai War of 1956.

Fatah and other Palestinian fedayeen groups might have remained in obscurity were it not for two developments—the collapse of the Egyptian-Syrian merger in 1961 and the completion of Israel's irrigation project—that had a decisive impact on the Arab world and the extremist element of the Palestinians.

After Israel's Sinai campaign of 1956, the Arab world persuaded itself that Egypt's defeat was due to the intervention of Britain and France. Israel's eventual defeat, the Arab press and radio reasoned, would only come about through the unification and concentration of Arab forces. The ideal of Arab unity began to catch on among the Arab nations and reached a fulfillment of sorts in the union of Syria and Egypt in 1958 into a new entity officially known as the United Arab Republic. Among Arab intellectuals and political thinkers there was discernible the feeling that this was the beginning of the path to true unity and an eventual Arab renaissance which would see the freeing of Palestine from Israel. The Palestine question became the focal point of the program for Arab unity and a rallying cry for all Arab and Moslem nations. The liberation of Palestine was raised at meetings of the Arab league and soon became a political football with rival nations accusing each other of inaction and indifference in the face of Palestinian refugee suffering.

The failure of the Cairo-Damascus experiment led men like Yasir Arafat, Fatah's future leader, and his colleagues to realize that the Palestinian people could not expect the Arab states to willingly act on behalf of a Palestinian entity since they were too embroiled in ideological disputes to act in coordination. Disappointment became a principal catalyst for a new breed of militants among the Palestinians. Yasir Arafat argued that if the Palestinians waited for Arab unity they would miss their chance. He developed the idea that rather than Arab unity being the precondition for the liberation of Palestine, it was the other way around: unless Palestine was liberated there could be no unification of the Arab people.

Arafat and his supporters found encouragement for their views in a speech delivered by President Nasser of Egypt to the Constitutional Council of Gaza in 1962. With candor, Nasser told the gathered Palestinians that he had no formula for liberating Palestine. To those Palestinians who were already thinking along the lines of independent action his speech was a final confirmation of what they had suspected for a long time. Arafat and others decided that the time had come to impel the Arab nations, no matter how unwilling, toward conflict with Israel. But even though the crisis in Arab unity was a major factor in determining Palestinian action, it was not of itself a crisis of sufficient magnitude to effect a direct response.

A second and more determinative crisis was, however, imminent and would lead to the actual formation of the fedayeen organizations. To understand the background of this development it is necessary to go back to the early 1950s when Israel began drafting a plan to tap the waters of the Jordan River based on her right as a riparian state under international law.

The original plan was to divert the Jordan at its upper course, before it enters the Sea of Galilee. In addition to supplying water via a system of conduits to the drought-ridden Negev, the diversion would have also made possible the operation of a hydroelectric power station.

The problem was that the Jordan does not flow only through Israel. About half of it lies in Jordan, as does its largest tributary, the Yarmuk River. Furthermore, in the north three sources feed the Jordan River. The major source, the Dan, rises in Israel. The other two sources, the Hasbani and Banyas, rise in Lebanon and Syria respectively.

Israel had earlier proposed a joint regional water scheme, but the Arabs, pursuing a policy of "what is good for Israel is bad for the Arabs," refused to participate. Nor was the need pressing for either Syria or Lebanon since they both possessed vast unused water sources, including springs and the Euphrates, Litani, and other rivers.

In 1953, Israel, eager to offset the effect of years of drought by tapping some of the Jordan's annual flow of almost a million gallons of water, began a hydroelectric project in the demilitarized zone near the Syrian border as the first step toward a southbound water conduit.

Syria's opposition brought the matter to the Security Council where the Arabs argued that since the point where Israel intended to take water from the Jordan River was situated in the demilitarized zone, Israel had no right to do this without Arab consent. Furthermore, they claimed, the digging of a diversionary canal gave Israel a military advantage and was therefore a violation of the 1948–1949 armistice agreement.

Israel pointed to the vast water resources available to the Arabs and argued that ninety percent of the waters of the Jordan-Yarmuk rivers were in Arab hands and were upstream of Israel's project.

The Security Council did not rule on the question but ordered Israel to stop all digging pending an enquiry. In January, 1954, a resolution sponsored by the United States, France and Britain, which might have led to a resumption of work on Israel's project, was supported by a majority of the Security Council but was vetoed by the Soviet Union. In the meantime, Jordan had formulated her own water project involving the diversion of the sweet-water Yarmuk from emptying into the Jordan and thereby greatly increasing the salinity of the water available to Israel. The United Nations drew up a third water scheme but neither side adopted it.

Israel nevertheless resumed work on her project but was persuaded to cease operations by the Eisenhower Administration's threat of cutting off economic aid. President Eisenhower had earlier sent Ambassador Eric Johnston to the Mideast for the purpose of drawing up a unified plan which would integrate all of the other plans' positive features. The U.S. Government promised financial support for the implementation of such a unified plan.

Underlying this search for a regional plan was recognition of the fact that each of the states on an international river system has a right to a portion of the water of that system. Israel, Jordan, Syria, and Lebanon are riparian states with regard to the Jordan River, while Jordan,

Syria, and Israel have similar status with regard to the Yarmuk River.

After three years of research, planning, and negotiation, Johnston reached an understanding with experts representing Jordan, Syria and Lebanon on the one hand, and Israel on the other, for a unified water plan. It covered basic factors such as the equitable allocation of the waters of the Jordan and Yarmuk among the respective states and the siting of storage and diversion installations. The Johnston plan took cognizance of Arab objections and demands and endorsed the water allocations for both Lebanon and Syria prescribed by an Arab technical committee. Jordan was also allocated sufficient water for irrigating her lands. The Johnston blueprint, which came to be known as the Unified Water Plan, was clearly designed to preclude any conceivable Arab claims or reservations at a later date.

Israel announced her acceptance of the plan, which as finally worked out gave her forty percent of the water of the Jordan River system, including the Yarmuk. Lebanon, Syria and Jordan were allocated the remaining sixty percent. After Arab technical experts approved the provisions of the U.W.P., the Arab League, meeting in Cairo in October, 1955, deferred consideration and thus its formal consent. The League explained its position on the grounds that the execution of the plan would involve indirect cooperation with Israel and would benefit the enemy's economy. It did not object to the fairness of the plan, but to any project that recognized Israel's existence.[1]

As the work on Israel's water carrier again advanced, the Arab states threatened to forcibly prevent Israel from continuing the hydraulic program. The controversy developed into another major political crisis as the Israeli waterworks neared completion and the time came for the Arabs to make good their threats.

Insofar as Nasser was concerned, the propaganda war would have to remain just that. With a large part of his army diverted to the side of the Republican forces in the Yemeni civil war, the Egyptian leader was in no position to embark on another military adventure. To his confidants he reportedly said: "When I begin a war, I want to achieve total victory, nothing less. Anyone can start a war, but only the victor can end it on his terms. I will not allow a war to begin unless I am one hundred percent sure of complete success."

In order to assuage widespread discontent in the Arab camp and restrain the volatile Palestinian extremists, Nasser called for a summit conference of Arab heads of state to convene in Cairo in January, 1964. As a precautionary move Nasser invited Ahmed Shukairy, who was then the Palestinian delegate to the Arab league.

The summit took place as scheduled with sixteen Arab leaders in attendance. In accordance with Nasser's wishes, the conference voted not to engage in a war with Israel because of the irrigation project. It was decided, instead, to undertake a grandiose hydraulic scheme aimed at depriving Israel of a considerable amount of the Jordan River's waters by altering the course of the Banyas River in Syria so that instead of feeding the Jordan, it would be brought over the watershed to empty into the Yarmuk in Jordan. A Lebanese engineering team was appointed and massive excavation equipment was leased from a Yugoslav company.

Work on this fantastic scheme, involving the altering of a river's natural course, began in the Golan Heights but was interrupted several times by Israeli air strikes. The Israeli attacks were in the form of reprisals for Syrian bombardment of Israeli agricultural settlements located in the Jordan valley below. Israel was able to pinpoint the location of the diversionary works, thanks to the work of intelligence operatives in Syria.

Yasir Arafat and other militant Palestinians were not convinced by the League's actions and saw the summit's decision as another example of the unwillingness of the Arab states to respond to the challenge of Israel's "expropriation of Arab waters" by going to war. This crisis of confidence was even greater than the depressed mood that followed the dissolution of the Egyptian-Syrian union. The Palestinians saw that they could only rely on themselves to revive the cause of Palestine's liberation.

By the summer of 1964, Israel's water carrier was in full operation and the Arab propaganda machine went into high gear. The second Arab summit was convened in the fall in Alexandria, Egypt, and this time Nasser sought to allay the noticeable ferment among the activist Palestinians. He hoped to provide an outlet for their frustration that Egypt could control. Accordingly, the summit created the Palestine Liberation Organization and a military arm—The Palestine Liberation Army—to be composed of units from each Arab country. Nasser was trying to institutionalize the Palestinian organizations and Shukairy as head of the P.L.O. was expected to adhere to guidelines set by Egypt.

Dissatisfaction increased among the Palestinians who regarded the summit's action as only token support for their cause. Arafat drew up a program for the nascent Fatah organization based on the following reasoning: the Arab states do not want war with Israel at this time. Time is on the side of Israel and not the Arabs. The balance of power tips every year further toward Israel and rumors that Israel is developing nuclear weapons only serve to reinforce this view. Amid these developments the Palestine question is neglected—the Arabs become accustomed to a problem without a solution and the world forgets the Palestinians. There is no alternative but to arouse the Palestinians by means of a new military offensive. It is necessary to initiate terrorist actions against Israel. These will not destroy her, but will weaken her militarily and economically. Above all, the terrorism will force Israel to retaliate against the Arab nations and these reprisals will eventually result in an all-out war neither side wants.

Within a short time, Fatah, with the active assistance of Syria, succeeded in inflaming the entire Middle East. A series of steadily intensified fedayeen attacks on civilian objectives were launched from bases in Syria. Because of Israel's acute sensitivity to Arab provocations, reprisals were sharp and served to escalate the spiral of terrorist outrages. Tension mounted along the Syrian border and instead of restraint, Syria responded to Israeli reprisals by openly declaring support for Fatah. In October, 1966, the United States, the Soviet Union and France persuaded Israel to place the matter before the Security Council instead of relying on military action. After six weeks of sterile debate, the Council failed to agree on any action, not even a resolution that might have assuaged Israel's feelings.[2] At this point, Russia began a diplomatic maneuver that was to seriously backfire. The Kremlin recognized an opportunity in Syria, which by means of the Fatah attacks on Israel was displaying increased belligerence. Russia was disappointed by Nasser's refusal to permit Communist political activity in Egypt despite large-scale economic and military aid provided by the Soviet Union. Nasser's appeal as a leader in the Arab world had been diminished by his costly and unsuccessful attempt to impose a new regime on Yemen. Nasser, in the Kremlin's eyes, was faltering in his drive to take over the Arabian peninsula and gain control of Middle East oil. Syria, although volatile and unstable, was further along the road toward Communism because of the leftist Baath party in power. There were close ties between the Baath party and the Soviet Communist party.

To exploit the political advantages offered by Syria's extremism, Moscow had to first effect a reconciliation between Syria and Egypt which were in conflict over ideological aims. The Syrians continually attacked Nasser for failing in his duty toward the liberation of Palestine by hiding behind the United Nations' peace-keeping force stationed in Sinai as a buffer between Egypt and Israel.

Russia worked to bring Egypt and Syria together and prevailed upon Nasser to move toward the more radical position of the Syrian leftists. As a result of Russian efforts, a meeting of Egyptian and Syrian leaders took place in Moscow in November, 1966. They agreed to resume diplomatic relations and drew up a treaty for joint defense that provided for each side to come to the aid of the other in case of attack. Thus the groundwork was laid for a succession of events, which contrary to Soviet expectations, led to the Six-Day War.

Increased Syrian belligerence resulted in fighting along the Syrian-Israeli border. In April, 1967, six Syrian MIGS were shot down by Israel. On May 12 Israel warned the Syrians of drastic reprisals if they continued to support Fatah attacks. At this point, Moscow saw a way to further her risky diplomatic gambit and her ambassador in Tel Aviv charged that Israel had mobilized forces along the Syrian border. Israel denied the charge and invited the Soviet ambassador to visit the border area and convince himself, but he refused. United Nations' observers and foreign correspondents visited the border and reported no mobilization. Moscow persisted in her allegations because an invasion threat to Syria provided Nasser with the pretext needed to come to the aid of Damascus.[3] The next step was to overcome the presence of the U.N. force and Nasser asked for its removal on May 18. At the same time, Egypt was massing forces in Sinai. Both Russia and Egypt were surprised by U Thant's immediate acquiescence in Nasser's request and suddenly the U.N. was out of Sinai and Sharm el Sheikh, which guarded the approach to the Straits of Tiran. The inevitable next step in the inexorable scenario was blockading the straits to Israeli shipping. Despite U.S. and British promises of action to lift the blockade nothing happened and Israel, feeling threatened and surrounded by hostile nations, put into effect plans for a pre-emptive strike. In six days the Arab forces were virtually destroyed and Israel had advanced to the Suez Canal and Jordan.

Eight years of no-war, no-peace had erupted in violence and the world saw how the actions of a small number of daring, ruthless men succeeded in creating circumstances for a general conflagration. Fatah's unbridled assaults on Israel and the maneuverings of the Soviet Union had exploited the Arab-Israeli conflict and paved the way to the Six-Day War. It was a war that the Arab states, with the possible exception of Syria, and Israel were drawn into against their will. The Arabs brought to the brink by precipitous actions setting off an inescapable and rapid flow of events, and Israel responding because of her hypersensitivity to anything threatening her existence.

NOTES

1. For a description of Johnston's experiences, see his account in The New York Times Sunday Magazine of October 19, 1958.
2. For a critique of Israeli government policy during this period see: Jon Kimche, *The Second Arab Awakening*, (New York: Holt, Rinehart & Winston, 1970) pp. 231–233.
3. A concise account of the Soviet role in the events leading up to the Six-Day War is provided by Benjamin Shwadran, "Soviet Posture in the Middle East," in *The Middle East Yesterday and Today*, eds. David W. Miller and Clark D. Moore (New York: Bantam Books, 1970) pp. 219–221.

CHAPTER 3

A Tradition of Terror

The appearance of Fatah and other fedayeen saboteur groups in the late 1960s was not the first time the Arabs had attempted guerrilla warfare against the Jewish settlement in Palestine. Terrorism has always been the chief method of local Arab opposition to the Jewish entity in Palestine, which was regarded with suspicion as a foreign intrusion, rather than the return of a people to its ancestral land. Since the days of Zionist settlement in the late nineteenth century, the Arab marauder, riding forth to burn and pillage villages and kill civilians has been a familiar figure in the Palestinian landscape.

The use of terror and irregular warfare is rooted in a

long-standing Arab tradition of combat. With the exception of Islam's period of great conquests in the seventh and eighth centuries, when tough desert fighters imposed the Prophet Mohammed's religious revelation on less-developed peoples, the Arab has not distinguished himself as a member of a regular fighting force.

Once the conquering desert Arabs began assimilating among the subjugated peoples, their fighting capability degenerated. No longer were the great warriors of Islam Arabs; their places were taken by Turks and members of other nations, including Christian youth forcibly converted to Islam. The Arabs have never emerged from this military decline and modern-day attempts by Arab nations to mold effective fighting forces have failed despite the enormous amount of arms and matériel made available to them on generous terms by the Soviet Union and the United States.

For many centuries, the Arabs have done better as *fedayeen*, solitary fighters, dagger-carrying, hit-and-run type warriors. The term *fedayeen* is the Arabic word commonly used for irregulars, but the concept of fedayeen action emphasizes the sacrificial aspect. It refers to the man who is willing to risk his life in carrying out his mission. The word fedayeen comes from the Arabic for sacrifice: *feda.* Thus, fedayeen are those who sacrifice themselves or assume a suicidal mission. The term fedayeen became well-known in modern times in 1955 when Egypt organized and sent into Israel squads of saboteurs and terrorists. In the twelfth century those selected to assassinate the enemies of the Ismaili sect were called fedayeen. In Europe these religious murderers were referred to as *assassins,* a Europeanization of the Arabic word for hashish, which the killers were accustomed to smoking before setting out on their missions.

Fedayeen

The Arab fighting man is uncomfortable in group endeavor and lacks developed feelings of solidarity toward his comrades in arms. Pulling together selflessly for a common purpose is not an Arab trait. They are incapable of prolonged and persistent cooperation and generally there is little cohesion among them. Social consciousness, allegiance toward the state and identification with leaders are not characteristics one can associate with Arabs.[1] Although the Palestinians have achieved a degree of unity, at least in their view of themselves in relation to the rest of the world, they share the common Arab mistrust of leaders and lack of faith in them. It is thus difficult to develop fighting élan and esprit de corps and the Palestinian fedayeen demonstrate this by their readiness to inform on each other without being pressured and their tendency to abandon wounded comrades.

The Arab inclination toward terrorism and guerrilla warfare is a result of an inability to effectively wage open warfare. In the context of the contemporary Arab-Israeli conflict, waves of Arab terrorism followed wars in which Arab regular armies suffered decisive defeats. After the 1948 war, Arab harassment of Israeli border settlements increased steadily, climaxing in the waves of Egyptian-sponsored fedayeen in 1955 and 1956. Before and after the Six-Day War, the Arabs put their trust in guerrilla and terrorist action.

As early as the 1880s, when Palestine was under Ottoman rule, the Jewish population, numbering a few tens of thousands, was subjected to onslaughts of robbery, marauding, murder, and rape. In 1886, a mob of Arab peasants tried to destroy Petah Tikva, an early Jewish settlement near Tel Aviv, but were beaten back by the settlement's defenders. Two years later, a large-scale Arab attack on a farm in Gedera was carried out and in ensuing years the handful of Jewish settlements and villages and communities in the Arab cities were terrorized by armed assaults.

These attacks were characterized by the use of rifles and daggers, the burning and destruction of crops and fields and by sniping. The sudden, devastating attacks were similar to the pogroms suffered by the Jewish communities in Poland and Russia for centuries. The Jews looked to the Ottoman authorities for protection but were disappointed. They learned to depend upon themselves for the protection of their lives, families, property, and even their right to live in the Holy Land. By the turn of the century, various embryonic military organizations with political leanings had been organized by Jewish settlers. Of these the most important was *Hashomer* (The Watchman), which became the forerunner of the Haganah, the underground Jewish self-defense group organized some years later by the Zionist leadership. These Jewish defense groups assumed the responsibility of protecting isolated villages and farming communities.

During the First World War, many young Palestinian Jews joined Jewish volunteers from Britain and America in the Jewish Legion, a fighting unit within the British Army. It provided young Jews with their first opportunity to receive real military training and to learn something of army organization.

The tension between Arabs and Jews assumed a more political character following the 1917 Balfour declaration in which Britain recognized the right of the Jews to establish a homeland in Palestine. Palestine was placed under a British Mandate granted by the League of Nations following the defeat of Turkey in World War I. Subsequently, Arab rejection of any program aimed at affording the Jews a national presence in a land that had been under various foreign rulers for centuries was expressed in three major outbreaks of terrorism: 1921, 1929, and 1936–39.

In 1921, the "Arab riots," as the attacks on Jewish settlements and centers of population came to be known, were aimed at both discouraging the Zionist enterprise and pressuring the British to alter their favorable attitude toward the notion of a Jewish national homeland. Although Arab hostility was confined at first to a small section of the Arab community it was fanned by the Arab nationalist movement that sought to oust the foreign mandatory powers and join Palestine to Syria to form an independent Arab kingdom. The anti-Zionist disorders took on the complexion of a political and religious struggle. The slogans *Itbahu al yahud!* (Slaughter the Jews) and *Falastin bladna wa al yahud clabna* (Palestine is our land and the Jews our dogs) were heard for the first time.

The extremism of the Arabs shocked many members of Palestine's Jewish settlement and relegated to myth the idea that the Arabs were willing to live peacefully with their Jewish neighbors.

From Jerusalem acts of terrorism spread to Jaffa, the Arab seaport north of Tel Aviv. Long-time Jewish residents, involved in the commercial and social life of Jaffa, and the Jewish newcomers to Palestine were murdered. From Jaffa this first wave of terror struck in Petah Tikva, Hadera, Rehovot, and other Jewish settlements and erupted in Jerusalem again. The Jewish community in Palestine emerged from this first experience with violent Arab opposition determined to take measures to protect itself against recurrences of similar terror and to develop economic institutions that would make it less dependent on the Arabs.

In 1929, a second campaign of Arab terrorism broke out, more intense and destructive than the first. The spark that ignited the outbreak was a religious dispute arising out of the refusal of the Arab authorities in Jerusalem to allow Jews to pray during the High Holy days at the most sacred site in Judaism—the Western Wall, a remaining fragment of Solomon's Great Temple, which adjoins a compound of mosques sacred to Islam.

In defiance of the Moslem religious authorities' prohibition, a group of Jews worshipped at the Western Wall on Aug. 23, 1929, and were attacked by an Arab gang shouting, "Allah and Mohammed command the killing of the Jews."

A few days later, an Arab mob murdered fifty-nine Jews in Hebron. The massacre was described in an eyewitness account in the London Times of Friday, August 30, 1929:

> The first house attacked was a large Jewish house on the main road, and the occupants locked themselves in. For some unknown reason the gates were opened to allow two young boys to leave, and they were immediately killed. This inflamed the crowd, who entered the house and beat or stabbed the inmates to death. The local police force, which consisted of only a British officer, two Arab officers and thirty Arabs, made every effort to control the situation, but the crowd was out of hand, and attacked other Jewish homes, beating and stabbing the inhabitants—men, women, and children. The police fired, but the situation was not definitely in hand until the arrival of twelve British police and twelve Royal Air Force personnel from Jerusalem.

In addition to Hebron, the historic Jewish community of Safed in northern Palestine was hit hard by Arab terrorists. Following the violence of 1929, the Jewish communities in the Arab cities of Nablus, Gaza, Tulkarem, Jenin, and Bet Shaan were abolished, the Jews having learned that their greatest security was in banding together in all-Jewish settlements and neighborhoods.

The Jews suffered greatly in 1929 but the Arabs failed to bring about their total annihilation because of the presence of the British who sometimes intervened to establish peace and order. The British could not always reach beleaguered areas and the Jews resolved to strengthen their own defense arrangements. Gradually the network of informal defense groups were merged into the unified Haganah.

In April, 1936, the third wave of Arab terrorism began and it was to be the most drastic yet. It is known as the "Arab revolt" and was aimed against British authority as well as the Jewish settlement. A key figure in the 1936 uprising was the pro-Nazi Grand Mufti of Jerusalem, Amin El Husseini. He exploited hatred of the Jews and Moslem religious fanaticism to inflame Arab emotions. Arab terrorist organizations, inspired by the Mufti, carried on a sustained guerrilla campaign in the name of religion. One of these groups named "Fighters of the Holy War" called on the local Arabs to become fedayeen, i.e.; sacrifice themselves for the sake of Allah. Those who fell were promised a place in heaven. In Fatah publications these religious warriors have been cited as ideological forerunners, examples to be emulated.

The Arab revolt began in 1936 in the urban centers and then spread to the villages. The city Arabs, however, quickly abandoned the struggle to their lesser-educated, rural brothers who attacked non-Arab vehicles traveling Palestine's roads and formed into guerrilla bands whose favorite targets included the pipeline carrying British-owned petroleum from the Kirkuk fields in Iraq to Haifa port. The guerrillas were commanded in a rather loose and haphazard manner by a Syrian army officer named Fawzi Kaoukji who had been dispatched by Syrian nationalist extremists to press the Arab reaction in Palestine against both the Jews and the British.

The British army's initial response to the Arab guerrilla bands in 1936 was ambiguous. Although heavy casualties were inflicted on the Jewish community, the British forces often showed themselves unwilling to suppress the wave of violence. The British Foreign Office feared that drastic action would turn the entire Arab Middle East against Britain at a crucial time and Whitehall was mindful of the inroads Nazism had made among rightist Arab political groups in Egypt. Only later, when the Arab revolt was well underway, did the British Army receive authorization to effectively put down the rebellion.

The Haganah realized both the danger to life and property the new situation represented as well as the implicit political threat. It was clear that under the circumstances the neutrality of the British and their occasional indirect support of the Arabs would undermine the Jewish presence in certain parts of the country and a reversal of Britain's commitment to the Balfour declaration. At first, the leaders of the Jewish settlement were in favor of defensive actions in the face of Arab hostility because it was assumed that the British would eventually intervene in the Jews' favor. Seventy percent of the Jewish community at that time lived in the three major cities of Tel Aviv, Haifa and Jerusalem. The remainder were in fortified agricultural settlements and villages. The nature of Jewish defense was static. The settlers tended to garrison themselves and large areas of property and fields were abandoned to marauding Arabs.

The military initiative was in Arab hands, but despite this tactical advantage they made a number of serious errors in the 1936–39 period. Not a few of their commanders mistakenly exaggerated the power of their own forces and minimized the potential of the Jews. The clashes of 1936 were between two nationalities and the Arabs were mistaken in directing their hostility against the British too. The latter were preoccupied with the deteriorating international situation. It was natural, therefore, that the British authorities would be in need of the Jewish community's cooperation, even if this meant military collaboration with the illegal Haganah.

Faced with the prospect of civil chaos and alarmed by attacks on the Iraqi Petroleum Company's pipeline, the British embarked on an offensive to suppress the Arab guerrilla fighters. Severe punishment was imposed on terrorist gangs and the local Arab population. Hardly a search of Arab communities was held without several civilians being killed and hundreds of homes, vineyards and orchards destroyed by the angry British troops and Palestine Police both as revenge and deterrent measures. To prevent infiltration by Arabs from neighboring countries the British set up watchtower police stations and fences in frontier areas. A further British measure was the occupation of twenty-five Arab villages in the Galilee to the north and the West Bank of the Jordan River in the middle of 1938. This was done to prevent supplies from reaching guerrilla and terrorist groups.

Steps were taken to strengthen the Jewish self-defense effort and these were to contribute greatly to the development of the Haganah, which was illegal because of British restrictions on Jews bearing arms. The first official action was the establishment of the Palestine Supernumerary Police. Thousands of Jewish men and women enrolled in this auxiliary force known also as the Jewish Settlement Police. The force was charged with the task of defending remote settlements and in this way thousands of Jewish settlers received their first training in the use of arms. At its high point the Supernumerary Police numbered some 22,000 men and women equipped with about 8000 rifles and other small arms and organized into guard and mobile units. Many of the Jewish police were also members of the still clandestine Haganah.

A second significant British initiative was the formation of the Special Night Squads of mixed Jewish and English units. This was actually an unofficial undertaking by Captain Orde Wingate, anxious to enlist Jewish help in protecting the IPC pipeline under attack by Arab guerrillas. Wingate cooperated with Haganah units in carrying out night-time raids and ambushes over wide areas of the Galilee on both sides of the pipeline. In the morning, the technically illegal Haganah units would disappear while the legal units returned to their bases. Dressed in blue shirts and Australian bush hats, the night fighters under Wingate's command helped drive Fawzi Kaoukji's guerrillas from the Galilee, away from the petroleum pipeline. Orde Wingate gave Yigal Allon, Moshe Dayan and other future Israeli army commanders their first formal instruction in warfare, particularly counter-guerrilla tactics. Dayan greatly admired Wingate and throughout his career has been influenced by the Englishman's emphasis on striking at the center of enemy activity rather than assuming a static defense. Wingate's example inspired the Haganah to begin attacking instead of limiting itself to defensive guarding tactics. A new operational method, employing mobile patrol units, went into effect and soon offensive strikes took place in confirmation of Wingate's maxim that the best defense is attack. This philosophy was later to become one of the primary combat doctrines of the Israel Defense Forces.

The advent of Orde Wingate was of historic importance for the Haganah and the fledgling Jewish settlement. Raised in the tradition of English Dissenters and Puritans, Wingate knew the Bible intimately and regarded its prophecies as the plain and simple truth. He saw the Jewish people and their struggle to return to the Land of Israel as a just and righteous cause and he dedicated himself to making the Haganah an effective fighting instrument. He was a man of brilliance, reserved and disciplined. He often quoted the Bible and saw himself as a modern Gideon, operating in the same terrain where the Biblical Gideon fought the Midianites. He instilled in the men of the Haganah a sense of mission and professionalism. His word was law and he insisted on meticulous discipline. Although he prepared every operation thoroughly, he was gifted in improvisation and trained his men to respond resourcefully to changing battle conditions. As a commander, he set a personal example in courage and endurance and regarded the men in his command as partners in thinking and action. The members of the Haganah thought of him as one of themselves and he was known affectionately as *Hayedid* (the friend). Together with Yitzhak Sadeh, the Haganah's legendary commander and strategist, Wingate was a decisive factor in shaping the armed Jewish response to Arab terror. Wingate's involvement with the Jewish underground provoked the displeasure of his superiors and he was transferred from Palestine.

Due to the Arab offensive, the Haganah achieved a remarkably high degree of centralized control in the uncertain circumstances of those prewar years. The events of 1936–39 brought about drastic changes in the attitude of the Jews of Palestine. New methods of military planning and organization came forth to prepare the Jews for an eventual all-out war. The erosion of British support for

Zionism as evidenced in the publication of a 1939 White Paper putting Britain on record as opposing continued Jewish immigration to Palestine, and the Munich Chamberlain-Hitler pact persuaded David Ben-Gurion and several other Jewish leaders of the folly of depending on the British and of the need for a long-range military strategy aimed at eventually replacing the Haganah with a national army in the conventional sense. An overall plan was devised for controlling and defending most of Palestine in the event of a British evacuation. A new approach in the pattern of settlement was instituted to answer the demands of the specific political and strategic circumstances imposed by the fierce Arab resistance to any type of permanent Jewish entity. There was an intensive effort to draw the outlying villages and farming settlements of the Jews into a unified national body with a presence in every sector of Palestine so that any future partition of Palestine would not cut off any outposts.

The Haganah, rapidly becoming a major factor in the programs and aspirations of the Zionist leaders, set up a special department for planning the defense of outlying areas. Civilian garrisons, known as "tower-and-wall" settlements sprung up in various sectors and were linked by a network of roads built under constant Arab harassment. In the three-year period of the Arab revolt fifty-two new settlements came into being and armed detachments of Jewish settlers returned to communities which had earlier been abandoned.

As the Arabs found their attacks to be increasingly costly, their initiative gradually diminished until a relative peace was achieved toward the spring of 1939. The Jewish settlement had survived and the military objective of driving the Jews out of Palestine had failed. But the Arabs scored definite political victories, namely the White

Paper of 1939. The British had realized that the Mandate was unworkable and that it could not be applied without large-scale and constant use of force against the Arabs. On the other hand, the migration of German and Central European Jews to Palestine following Hitler's rise to power—by 1937 the Jewish population in Palestine was 400,000 as compared to 175,000 in 1932—made it equally difficult to reverse the moral-legal obligation to help establish a Jewish National Home as implied in the Balfour Declaration. Failing to achieve a settlement of the Palestine question by agreement in a special conference of Arabs and Jews, the British sought a way to retain Arab good will which they believed was crucial to the war effort in the Middle East. They settled on the issuance of the White Paper, which was practically a reversal of the Balfour Declaration and severely restricted Jewish immigration and property acquisition. Jewish resistance to the White Paper policy was minimal during World War II as the Haganah joined in the anti-axis war effort.

By the time World War II was over, however, the British were actively backing the Arabs in opposing the establishment of a Jewish state. Some members of the British Government feared Soviet penetration of the Middle East and felt a cordon sanitaire of Arab states offered a buffer against Soviet expansionism.

Jewish resistance to the British intensified and some dissident Jewish underground units launched several terrorist attacks against British installations and personnel. At the same time, international opinion on the side of the Jews began to be felt as revelations of the Nazi holocaust came out. The pressure on the British to permit massive immigration of the concentration camp survivors increased just as the postwar Arab nationalist movement was agitating against continued British presence in the

Middle East and the Zionist aim of establishing a sovereign state in a portion of Palestine.

The Arab revolt of 1936–39 had the effect of steeling the Jewish community for the future, but among the Palestinians the effect was the opposite. Instead of developing a fighting force during the years of World War II, the Arabs of Palestine fell into a state of apathy and did little more than maintain the status quo. Despite the sudden surge of religious and ethnic enthusiasm, the Palestinian Arabs had shown that they were unable to go beyond the fedayeen-type action to organized military operations which depend on a sense of national cohesion.

The White Paper was an apparent victory for the 1936–39 tactics of the Palestinians, but they allowed their nationalism to be co-opted by the larger issue of British control in the Middle East and were divided by various feuding Arab factions. Palestinian nationalism became an instrument of the Egyptians, the Hashemites, and the Syrians. The Palestinians were the pawns in the complicated intrigues and power politics of the postwar reaction against British colonialism. The leadership of the Palestinians fell into the hands of men who were financed and controlled by outside factions. The Mufti encouraged renewed terrorism directed against the Jews and moderate Arabs. He also forced the hand of the Arab nations and secured their pledges to go to war against any attempt to establish a Jewish state.

In 1947, the British, increasingly reluctant to be responsible for the explosive situation in Palestine, decided to relinquish their mandate. Following the United Nations resolution of November 29, 1947, providing for Jewish and Arab states in the disputed land, the Palestinian leaders, anticipating the forthcoming war, fled to Syria. Their example was followed by the Palestinian masses and some 500,000 to 600,000 left their homes to await the outcome of the war which their absent leaders assured them would see the annihilation of the Jews. The ensuing invasion by Arab forces and the war with newly established Israel determined the pattern of Arab-Jewish relations in the years to come. The Palestinian Arabs chose exile rather than face the Jews in open battle or live in peaceful coexistence with a Jewish state.

In the years following Israel's independence, the Arabs again employed terrorism as the instrument of their opposition to the new country, created by international consent and recognized by the United Nations. A new type of guerrilla offensive was mounted from neighboring Arab countries. Infiltrators would strike at civilian targets, killing women and children whenever possible. They would return to bases in countries across the border and remain there in safety until their next exploit. The lure of looting motivated these infiltrators more than political sentiment and eventually bands of fedayeen bandits carried out frequent outrages against Jewish settlements.

The intelligence units of Arab armies found that these irregulars could supply firsthand information on activities inside Israel. In return for permission to carry out looting raids, the terrorists were obliged to engage in a primitive form of espionage.

Israel was particularly vulnerable in border areas since large sections were unsettled and there was the danger that these would become no-man's land. As thousands of European Jews, survivors of the Nazi era, emigrated to Israel in the early 1950s many were moved into new border villages and semi-cooperative farms. They provided an easy and convenient target for the Arab infiltrators who were becoming a serious threat to the security and well-being of the infant state. Although Israel had managed to rebuff the established Arab armies, her military forces were not prepared for the new type of guerrilla offensive as it penetrated the long borders Israel shared with hostile Arab governments. The infiltrators went beyond frontier areas and struck cities in the interior as well as the Jewish sector of Jerusalem, which had been divided as a result of the 1948 war and was located in a corridor of Israeli land surrounded on three sides by Arab territory. Murders of civilians in Israeli towns and cities became daily occurences in Jerusalem and suburbs of Tel Aviv where Israel was a mere ten miles in diameter. Morale in the new nation suffered and the Israel Defense Forces were at a loss in coping with this new Arab challenge.

The nature of Arab terrorism after 1948 was essentially spontaneous and disorganized. Within a few years, however, a new brand of terrorism appeared on the Middle East scene. This was in 1955, when the word "fedayeen" began to be heard with increasing frequency. The reference was to the suicide squads of Arab assailants sponsored and equipped by Egypt. They used the Gaza Strip on Israel's southern flank as a launching base for murderous sorties on Israeli settlements. These fedayeen were often convicted criminals released from prison to serve Egyptian intelligence and act as tools of Nasser's policy of harassing Israel without exposing Egypt to the danger of an all-out war. Although Gaza was used as a base, Egypt also sought to involve other Arab states in a dispute with Israel and arranged for fedayeen to operate from Jordan and Lebanon.

The fedayeen reached new heights of daring and struck terror into the hearts of border settlers and civilian motorists traveling in frontier zones. The wanton killing of mothers and infants dismayed the nation and became a precipitating factor in the Sinai War of 1956. The fedayeen force numbered about 700 and was a regular fighting organization commanded by Egyptian officers and non-commissioned officers and housed in three army camps near the Mediterranean coast and in billets provided by civilians in Gaza. The fedayeen were paid a small monthly wage and promised a bonus for every mission carried out in Israel. Their families were promised compensation should any of them fall in action. Advanced training was given the fedayeen in Egypt and they were taught to operate in groups of two to seven men, infiltrating into Israel by night and returning to home base the following night. Each team was usually headed by a man who knew the target area well.

The fedayeen were given rigorous training and displayed a fairly high degree of physical coordination, but they had difficulty sticking to an assigned task and usually tried to avoid exposing themselves to danger. Favored fighting methods were the ambush or throwing hand grenades into homes. They rarely attacked areas protected by Israeli army units and would frequently hide among Israeli Arabs, often with relatives. Despite their successes and the considerable propaganda devoted to their exploits, few Israeli Arabs joined their ranks.

In 1956 this was the picture of fedayeen activity against Israel: twenty-six percent of the attacks consisted of throwing hand grenades and firing on civilian town settlements; twenty-three percent of the operations were ambushes directed mainly against civilian vehicles; sixteen percent of the fedayeen efforts resulted in the blowing up and sabotage of water installations and thirteen percent of the attacks involved passersby, mainly civilians on the street; nine percent were acts of destruction using explosives to blow up buildings and other installations; five percent mine-laying; sabotaging major highways represented another four percent of fedayeen operations and only four percent of the incidents involved were intended clashes with Israeli army patrols or watchmen.[2]

The tension along Israel's borders because of the fedayeen attacks became intolerable and contributed substantially to Israel's decision to launch a pre-emptive counterattack to put an end to border infiltrations. Further aggravating the delicate situation was Egypt's nationalizing of the Suez Canal and closing it to Israeli navigation. Egypt also imposed a blockade on Eilat-bound vessels in the Gulf of Aqaba. These moves seriously threatened Israel's security, sovereignty, and economic life. A series of retaliations carried out against enemy bases and border outposts failed to bring more than temporary relief from the fedayeen harassment. The concentration of Egyptian forces in northern Sinai, close to Israel's border, and the conclusion in October, 1956, of a military pact among Egypt, Jordan, and Syria, creating a single command, further alerted Israel to the dangers of a three-sided Arab invasion. The interest of Britain and France in regaining control of the Suez Canal created a favorable situation for an Israeli strike. A joint plan was worked out and on October 29 Israeli forces crossed into Sinai. By November 5 they occupied all of the peninsula with the exception of a ten-mile corridor along the Suez Canal. On November 5 British and French forces mounted a joint offensive against the Canal Zone, but called off their operation the next day because of U.S. and Soviet pressure. Israel subsequently was made to withdraw her troops from Sinai and they were replaced by a U.N. emergency force. Israel was given guarantees of freedom of navigation in Suez and the Gulf of Aqaba and a decade of quiet ensued in which neither Egypt nor Israel wanted unrest on their borders nor a major conflict. The Suez Canal was not opened to vessels flying Israeli flags but Israeli shipping moved freely through the Gulf of Aqaba to and from the Red Sea port of Eilat.

From the time of the Sinai War until the Six-Day War eleven years later, no terrorists operated from Egyptian territory. The resumption of Arab guerrilla war on a significant scale came in 1965 when Fatah began its struggle under Syria's patronage. This new stage in the ongoing Arab-Israel conflict was accompanied by slogans proclaiming the liberation of Palestine through a popular war of liberation. The renewed Arab thrust compared itself with other guerrilla struggles, e.g.; Greece's civil war after the Second World War in which Greek Communist guerrillas used neighboring Communist countries as bases and sanctuaries, and the Huk insurgency in the Philippines. Both of these examples, however, were failures. For the men of Fatah the war in Vietnam also became an important point of comparison and the Palestinians liked to describe themselves as the Middle Eastern version of the North Vietnamese and Vietcong fighting Western imperialism.

In the summer of 1966, General Moshe Dayan visited Vietnam as a special correspondent for several newspapers. Upon his return to Israel in the fall he remarked:

> The war in Vietnam is far larger than a guerrilla conflict. In Israel the infiltrators are waging a battle that is much smaller than a guerrilla war. In Vietnam men of Vietnamese nationality are opposing a foreign force—the American army. Many Vietnamese see the slogan, "Yankee Go Home" as a symbol of a policy based on the hope and belief that in the end the United States will tire of the American blood being spilled in a far-off land. In Israel the situation

is quite the opposite. The infiltrators are led and controlled by foreigners in a neighboring country. The policy of the infiltrators is determined in Damascus and Cairo and this policy is part of these nations' general considerations of which Israel is only one concern.

The fedayeen translated the works of leading guerrilla war theorists into Arabic and set these works as models for themselves. They did not, however, pay close attention to several principles enumerated in these books. For example, Mao Tse-tung clearly states in his treatise on guerrilla warfare, "Yo Tchi Tchian," that copying the methods of guerrilla warfare from another locale is doomed to failure because every nation possesses special situations and conditions peculiar to that area. The fedayeen motto of a "popular war of liberation" was based on the belief that only by means of guerrilla war would Israel be defeated. Mao states that guerrilla war is meant to represent only a transitory stage of conflict, leading eventually to a conventional war which is the only way to gain victory.

There is no precise definition of guerrilla war but its practical meaning is terrorism, subversion, and the struggle of bands of saboteurs carried out everywhere—at the front and behind the lines. The aim of guerrilla warfare is to cause maximum casualties and damage while avoiding direct combat. Every guerrilla war takes place in its own special circumstances, but certain basic factors determine the prospects for success. Three of the most important factors are the physical terrain of the embattled region, the population, and political conditions.

The ideal geography for guerrilla warfare is one with mountains and forests or forested swampy areas such as in

Vietnam. Successful examples of partisan and guerrilla action show that the terrain of conflict offered thick woods and other suitable hiding places where bases, supply lines and field hospitals could be clandestinely maintained. Before the Six-Day War, Israel was far from ideal as a site for guerrilla operations. The Negev desert was largely a barren waste, open to aerial and surface reconnaissance and offering practically nothing in the way of sanctuary or hiding places. The only area of Israel resembling the ideal was the northern Galilee. Adjoining the Syrian border and accessible to infiltrators from Lebanon and Jordan, the Galilee was semi-forested and contained many Arab villages. It was, however, a relatively small area of land and an efficient army could encircle it and comb it thoroughly with little difficulty. The Galilee was not a place large numbers of guerrillas could roam about in safety.

Unlike other armies who have had to fight guerrillas in unfamiliar locations, the Israeli forces were at home and knew the land better than the Palestinians, many of whom had never lived there. From the point of view of geography, guerrillas would find it difficult to establish bases in Israel. All bases would have to be set up in Arab territory and this would expose the host countries to Israeli retribution.

The population also offered few possibilities to the Syrians and Fatah. Without the aid of the local population guerrilla forces cannot succeed. Mao likens the guerrilla fighters to fish and the population to the life-sustaining sea. Without the cooperation of the civilians in the countryside, the insurgents would be unable to find hiding places, would lack adequate food, military intelligence, and a source of recruiting additional men. Fatah looked hopefully to the area of concentrated Arab population in Israel. But on the whole, Israeli Arabs chose not to assist Fatah. Some individuals did support Arafat's group in this period before the Six-Day War, but their help was limited to information-gathering and did not include participation in any attacks inside Israel. The lack of response on the part of Israel's indigenous Arab citizens made it unlikely that the Syrians and Fatah would achieve their aim of a broad-based guerrilla struggle.

Political conditions in the Middle East and the world were also not on the side of the Palestinian guerrillas. Egypt and the other members of the Arab League were anxious to avoid war with Israel and on the international level world opinion in 1965 opposed any worsening of the Arab-Israeli dispute. The fedayeen squads were still remembered as was the abortive Suez adventure of England and France in 1956. Furthermore, the Syrian Baathists were considered extremist and were criticized by a large portion of the world's moderate and anti-Communist press.

Israel had reason to believe that heavy retaliatory raids on her part against Syria would be understood in view of the fedayeen provocations inspired by that country. Israel's policy of retribution had undergone several definitions over the years as it evolved from the early Jewish settlers' philosophy of *havlagah* (restraint), in the face of Arab terrorism. In the years following the birth of Israel a policy of response to Arab provocation emerged based on the assumption that there was no possibility of deterring Arab aggression and harassment unless Israel replied with reprisals that would not only meet the degree of Arab provocation, but would be at least two-fold in severity. Only in this way would the Arabs begin to question the value of their actively hostile policy toward Israel. As the army tried to find its way in the planning and staging of reprisals military failures resulted. The army was forced on several occasions to turn to civilian reservists, veterans of the 1948 conflict, to carry out reprisals on an irregular partisanlike basis. Mishaps were frequent and eventually this system gave way to the formation of special, elite units which were specially trained for the most dangerous and vital missions. Israel's reaction was based on armistice agreements with the Arabs that stipulated that the nation from which the terrorist attacks were launched would bear responsibility. Jerusalem was determined that the Arab states would not evade blame for sponsoring the fedayeen.

Fighting terrorism with terrorism, Israel tried many of the methods used by the Arabs—houses were blown up, military and civilian vehicles were mined, and sniping and shelling were used as were occasional kidnappings. In the early 1950s units of the Israel Defense Forces were dispatched to neighboring Arab countries to carry out such terrorist tactics as blowing up wells and telephone lines and stealing livestock. But none of these efforts provided an overall solution to the problem of ending fedayeen murders and looting. The then Chief of Staff, Moshe Dayan, explained Israel's doctrine of retaliatory strikes by saying that Arab governments would restrain their own irregulars only after it became clear that the theft of one cow from a Jewish settlement would hurt an Arab village and that the murder of one Jew inside Israel would endanger the population of Gaza. In October, 1954, an unauthorized Israeli attack took place at the Jordanian village of Kfar Kibiya. More than fifty Arab civilians, including women and children, were killed. Official spokesmen said no regular Israeli army unit had been involved in the incident and hinted that the action might have been carried out by Israeli settlers angry over fedayeen harassment. A public outcry led to a government decision to prohibit actions against nonmilitary objectives. Now reprisals were directed solely against the military in the hope that Egypt would be persuaded to cease arming and dispatching fedayeen squads across the border and that Jordan would crack down hard on fedayeen originating on her territory. This new era of Jewish response began in the latter part of 1954 and reached its climax with the Sinai War in 1956.

Following the Sinai campaign, Israel modified her policy of limiting retribution to only military targets when she learned that as long as she used different methods of retribution and did not adhere to one method alone she succeeded in overcoming the enemy by surprise and was able to inflict heavy damage. When Israel limited herself to special targets, such as purely military objectives, she sustained a high rate of casualties. From the outset of guerrilla action against Israel, the dilemma of the Jews has always been the question of proportion. Should every Arab provocation be answered with an appropriate response or should Israel bide her time, launching heavy retaliations after a string of Arab raids? Discussion on the subject would cite the danger of entering into an unending spiral of attack-counterattack. The aim of Israel's response was to put an end to the threat of fedayeen hostility while avoiding a widening guerrilla war. The experience of dealing with Arab terror persuaded Israel that massive retaliations make a greater impression on the enemy and discourage further aggression. Because of this attitude Israel would collect a score of provocations before settling accounts in one, large reprisal action. Israel's world image suffered somewhat due to this policy because the large-scale response made headlines while the Arabs' singular acts of murder—even of women and children—often went unnoticed in the world press.

Israel's pattern of retribution until the Six-Day War gave her army experience but it did not completely stop fedayeen infiltration. Reprisal attacks demonstrated to the Arabs that they would have to pay a heavy price for violating Israel's borders and that Arab border areas were just as vulnerable as those of Israel's.

From the time Fatah began what it calls its "guerrilla war of liberation" against Israel until the Six-Day War, one hundred incidents of sabotage, attempted sabotage, and other terrorist actions took place on Israeli territory. The selection of targets shows a marked tendency to strike at civilian objectives. If the mining of border roads is considered a military objective, then more than ninety percent of the sites are civilian—wells, irrigation pipes, field pumping stations, dwellings, barns, and agricultural warehouses, tractors and other farm vehicles, railroad tracks, natural gas wells, electrical transformers, bridges, and a soccer field. While several of these incursions caused damage, not one raid during this period could be considered a major operation. In the two and a half years under discussion eleven Israelis were killed and sixty-two wounded as a result of fedayeen attacks. Fedayeen losses for this period are estimated at no more than ten.

What Fatah failed to achieve in their raids they nevertheless claimed in their announcements and proclamations. According to their claims, dozens of Israeli soldiers were killed and vital military installations destroyed as a result of their guerrilla combat. No matter how ridiculous their assertions, they had a narcotic, stirring effect on the Arab masses. Fatah's self-serving radio and press propaganda and wildly exaggerated reporting was to reach unprecedented heights following the Six-Day War, but even in this early period of activity the tendency to create a fedayeen myth was abundantly evident.

The pre-Six-Day War experience of Fatah was not a military success. Israel was able to withstand the fedayeen attacks but had to significantly increase her defense budget and extend the period of active military service for men to thirty months to do so. The net result of Israel's response was a moderate degree of success in arresting terrorist attacks achieved at considerable cost.

Fatah did attain its goal of bringing the Mideast to war and in the aftermath of the June, 1967, conflict the fedayeen found an opportunity to continue their war against Israel and the subversion of Jordan and Lebanon.

NOTES

1. Sania Hamady, *Temperament and Character of the Arabs*, (New York: Twayne Publishers, 1960) pp. 226–30.
2. Official Israeli government statistics.

CHAPTER 4

The Rise of Yasir Arafat and Fatah

In the years following the Arab defeat in Israel's 1948 War of Liberation, Palestinian terrorist groups appeared on the scene from time to time, only to disappear as suddenly as they emerged. For this reason Israeli intelligence did not pay undue attention to first reports of the formation of a new Palestinian fedayeen organization calling itself Fatah.

Systematic surveillance by Israeli security agencies of Fatah began at a later stage, when the group actually commenced its sabotage operations on Israeli soil.

The origins of Fatah are obscured because of its leadership's tendency to imbue the group with an aura of romantic mystery. The best available information indicates that the first attempts to organize Fatah took place in the Gaza Strip following its short-lived capture by Israel in the Sinai campaign of November, 1956. Many of Fatah's leaders come from Gaza, and others have close family ties to this arid, densely populated region, which until the Six-Day War was under Egyptian control.

Yasir Arafat, the rotund, usually unshaved chief of Fatah, has relatives living today in Gaza. They discuss their famous relative quite openly and have on more than one occasion even refuted some of Arafat's claims.

One of Arafat's cousins says that Yasir was not born in Jerusalem, as he maintains to enhance his image as a displaced Palestinian, but in Cairo in 1931, where his father moved in the 1920s. Yasir's complete name was Abd-el-Rahman Abd-el-Rauf Arafat el-Qud el-Husseini. He shortened it to conceal his kinship with the Mufti of Jerusalem, Haj Amin el Husseini, the discredited Palestinian leader who collaborated with the Nazis during World War II. Later Arafat took Abu Amar as a *nom de guerre* in honor of the first Moslem to fall in Mohammed's holy wars.

Arafat grew up in Cairo, where he displayed a religious bent, often expressing his Islamic fervor in sudden and passionate fits of religious righteousness. He joined the fanatic, right-wing *Ikhwan*, or Moslem Brotherhood, which preached a fundamentalist belief in Islam and deplored Western, modernizing influences on the Arab world.

The future Fatah leader began his political career in 1951 as an engineering student at Cairo University. He founded the Union of Palestinian Students in Egypt, an organization that had close ties to the Moslem Brotherhood. A sloppy, ascetic young man, Arafat had little to do with girls or other student diversions. He found companionship with fellow Palestinians, particularly those with ties to Gaza. As Palestinians, these young men felt outside of Egyptian society. Their frugal, marginal existence did much to forge a sense of camaraderie.

Several of the friends he made at this time later became Arafat's lieutenants in Fatah. Membership in the Moslem Brotherhood was suspect in the eyes of Egyptian authorities and as a Palestinian activist, Arafat was kept under constant surveillance by Nasser's secret police. Nevertheless, he served in a Palestinian unit of the Egyptian army and passed an officers' course in sabotage. In 1953 he was one of a band of saboteurs who carried out attacks against the British in the Suez Canal zone. In the 1956 Suez war Arafat was a Second Lieutenant.

An unsuccessful assassination attempt on Nasser's life resulted in the eradiction of the Moslem Brotherhood and by 1957 Arafat found the atmosphere in Egypt too repressive and left for the oil Sheikdom of Kuwait, where Palestinians were prominent in the petroleum industry. In Kuwait, Arafat prospered as a public works engineer, but his overriding concern was organizing guerrilla warfare against Israel. He found an encouraging response among Palestinian oil workers. His work was financed by wealthy Palestinians and in the middle of 1959 Arafat founded "Fatah," which is an acronym standing for the Arabic words *Haarakat Tahrir Falastin* (Movement for the Liberation of Palestine). The acronym was reversed since *HATAF* in Arabic connotes sudden death. FATAH means conquest.

Arafat and several friends moved to Beirut where they took control of *Our Palestine*, a small-circulation, religiously oriented newspaper published in Lebanon. In *Our Palestine*, Fatah expressed its views for the first time, but because it feared the Lebanese authorities, the leadership stayed underground and generally preferred anonymity. Arafat gave up engineering and thanks to a generous Palestinian supporter devoted himself full-time to traveling and speechmaking.

His single-mindedness impressed the Palestinians he came in contact with. His disdain for comfort and luxury and his abstinence from wine and sex were elements in a legend that soon grew up around him. Sympathetic Arab newspaper accounts have portrayed Arafat in saintly terms, ascribing to him such heroic characteristics as extraordinary courage, modesty, simplicity, and devotion to his followers. At least in one respect Arafat is truly remarkable and that is his ability to survive. He has eluded capture by Israel several times and has emerged uninjured from attempts on his life. In October, 1971, Arafat was fired on during an inspection tour of fedayeen positions in southern Syria. He was unharmed but his driver was killed. Arab sources said the attempt was carried out by a splinter Fatah group opposed to Arafat's attempts to negotiate a reconciliation with King Hussein of Jordan. The following anecdote is typical of Arafat survival legends:

He was once traveling through rough terrain in a Landrover loaded with arms and highly volatile explosives. A blowout caused the vehicle to swerve off the road and hurtle into a rocky wadi. Arafat, who was dozing, awoke with a start when the vehicle came to a halt. "What happened?" he asked.

"As you see," his driver replied, "we have come through without a scratch. If one hand grenade had gone off we would have been blown sky high!"

In his speeches and writing Arafat emphasized that the liberation of Palestine could not wait for the Arab states, which stifled the Palestinian urge for self-determination. At this stage Fatah contented itself with rhetoric and attempts to raise funds to keep its publication going. In 1961, Fatah consisted of no more than twenty active members.

As time went on, the organization grew bolder in its propaganda and emphasized the need for an armed struggle against Israel led by Palestinians and supported by Arab nations. The F.L.N.'s apparent success in Algeria against the French inspired Arafat and his comrades. They flatly rejected the view that the return of the Jews to their homeland could not accurately be compared to the French colonial presence in Algeria and that the success of the F.L.N. in ousting the French was due mainly to Charles de Gaulle's willingness to relinquish the colony.

With the coming of Algerian independence, Arafat traveled to north Africa where he was received warmly by a regime eager to gain status in the eyes of the world national liberation movements. Arafat opened a Fatah office in Algiers and obtained promises of training and support for future operations.

Algeria was not the only Arab country to come to the aid of Fatah in its early years. In 1963, the Baath Socialist Party seized power in Syria and it was only natural for Fatah's leaders to approach the leftist, revolutionary regime contending with Nasser of Egypt for the crown of Arab nationalism.

Syria was closer than Algeria to the area of conflict and actually bordered on Israel. The possibilities for receiving operational support from the new leaders in Damascus were virtually unlimited. The Syrians regarded the new Palestinian group as a sword for hire, a means of both needling Nasser and enhancing their own prestige in the Arab world.

From 1964 to 1966 Fatah received total Baath support. The initial acts of sabotage carried out by Fatah in 1965 surprised the Arabs, particularly Egypt, more than Israel. The lethargy of the Palestinians had been a long-established fact of life in the Middle East. Nevertheless, Egypt was quick to recognize the exceptional nature of Fatah. Here for the first time was a Palestinian organization attempting to live up to its slogans without fear of provoking established Arab leadership. From the outset of Fatah's active period Nasser was faced with a dilemma. As the leader of the Arab world, the Egyptian president feared that the fedayeen would eventually drag Egypt into another war with Israel—something Nasser wished to avoid. He was well aware of Israel's sensitivity to attacks and could be sure there would be fierce reprisals. Egypt would then either have to come to the aid of other members of the Arab League or admit to the world that she could not defend Arab countries.

Nasser was also concerned lest Syria dictate the tone of the Palestinian struggle and Egypt suffer a decline in prestige among Arab and Palestinian nationalists. Having weighed the courses open to him, Nasser apparently decided that the threat of Israeli reprisals outweighed other considerations and he ordered a ban on fedayeen attacks from Egyptian territory.

Before Nasser's ban went into effect, Fatah carried out three guerrilla raids from the Egyptian-controlled Gaza Strip. In February, 1965, Fatah agents placed mines on the Israeli border. Twice, the mines were discovered and disarmed; the third time they exploded, injuring seven members of an Israeli patrol. The Fatah men responsible for the three escapades were arrested on Nasser's orders and the fedayeen were warned that terrorist acts originating in Gaza or other Egyptian areas were outlawed. The border between Israel and Egypt remained quiet until the Six-Day War. Even in the middle of 1966, when Nasser reversed his policy regarding the fedayeen, he did not permit Palestinian guerrillas to operate from Egypt.

At first, Fatah's announcements were broadcast solely in Damascus and were regarded by most Arabs as part of the ongoing feud between the Baath party and Nasser. Although close relations developed between Fatah and Syria, the fedayeen group's main office was in Beirut and its first members were recruited at the refugee camps in Lebanon among men accustomed to hiring themselves out to the various Arab intelligence agencies.

Lebanon was particularly sensitive about Fatah activity as the nation bore painful memories of the 1958 civil war. Lebanese authorities sought to prevent their country from being used as a breeding ground for Palestinian and Moslem agitation. The Lebanese wanted to preserve their peaceful existence and enjoy the profits of tourism and other commercial pursuits.

Jordan was even more sensitive to fedayeen activity originating within its borders. For some time, Hussein had been contending with Egyptian and Syrian agents plotting against him and he regarded the extremist Palestinians, who aided these subversive elements, as a serious threat to his reign. The establishment of the Palestine Liberation Organization by the Arab League summit conference in January, 1964, had put Hussein on the alert against the Palestinian threat. The youthful king rejected proposals to establish Palestinian units in his army and refused to declare universal conscription. He claimed that Jordan's army was, in fact, Palestinian and there was no need to create separate units. He refused to permit the P.L.O. to operate in Jordan.

Fatah represented a more serious threat to Hussein

and his supporters, mostly desert bedouins, than Ahmed Shukairy's Egyptian-sponsored P.L.O. Arafat's group appeared extremist and irresponsible and it had the support of the equally irresponsible Baathists in Damascus. Hussein in 1965 probably feared Fatah more than Israel. His opposition took the form of intensive security and intelligence measures. The *mukthars*, or elders, of border villages were ordered to notify the authorities of the identity of anyone crossing the border to Israel. Jordanian security forces arrested many Arabs with criminal records who had served Egypt as fedayeen mercenaries during the 1950s.

In the first year of Fatah operations Jordan willingly accepted from Israel lists of Jordanians collaborating with the fedayeen group. Israeli intelligence kept a close watch on Jordanian border villages and on several occasions extensive arrests of Jordanians were made on the basis of lists received from the Jewish enemy. Usually these arrests resulted in short prison terms.

The increased tempo of terrorist raids provoked retaliatory strikes by Israel. In October, 1965, Hussein told the Jordanian Parliament in Amman that he would not support any Palestinian movement on Jordanian soil.

"Such organizations will give Israel an excuse to attack our people before we can adequately defend ourselves," he said.

Hussein's intentions notwithstanding, Fatah and other fedayeen bands continued launching attacks from Jordan, the Arab nation with the best proximity to Israel's populated areas. Syria and Egypt, however, did not allow the use of their territory for fedayeen operations.

Documents captured by Israel during the Six-Day War reveal that Palestinians suspected of membership in Fatah were kept under watch by Egypt's secret police as early as 1965. In that year Nasser's anti-fedayeen policy was shown in other ways. The Egyptian press conducted a campaign against Yasir Arafat, recalling his earlier association with the Moslem Brotherhood and labeling him a "Zionist" and an "imperialist," words Arafat often uses to denounce enemies. One paper wrote that the Fatah leader was "an agent of Zionism and imperialism sent to stir up trouble to give Israel an excuse for attacking the Arab states."

Nasser tried to discourage support for the fedayeen by making it a matter of general Arab consent. At the Arab summit in December 1965 in Casablanca, Morocco, Egypt introduced a resolution recommending that all acts of terrorism against Israel be halted for the time being and that no aid be given the fedayeen. The resolution was passed with Syria abstaining. A month later the Joint Arab Command, acting on the basis of resolutions passed by the Arab representatives to the Arab-Israeli Truce Commission, issued an order authorizing all nations bordering on Israel to prevent infiltrators from crossing the respective borders into Israel.

The justification for these actions was that the fedayeen violated the basic Arab strategy of preparing for all-out war against Israel at the appropriate time. The Egyptian newspaper, *Al Gumhoriya*, explained that there was no point in endangering the residents of border villages and exposing them to the danger of "barbaric" Israeli reprisals for the sake of permitting Fatah the privilege of conducting a few limited actions. At the same time, *Al Gumhoriya* called on the Arab states to adopt a more cordial attitude toward Fatah and to stop harassing its members.

The stance of the Arab governments on the fedayeen issue aroused strong opposition among several sectors of

Arab public opinion. A small number of inconclusive Fatah excursions had fired the Arab imagination and Arafat's group had gained a certain amount of fame and prestige which were only increased by Nasser and the Joint Arab Command's opposition to guerrilla attacks on Israel.

The Palestine Liberation Organization, which had been created in 1964 by the Arab summit conference, was at first obliged to oppose Fatah. Ahmed Shukairy, the vitriolic and aggressive Palestinian who at one time represented Saudi Arabia at the United Nations, regarded Fatah as a threat to his position as head of the P.L.O. In adopting a line similar to that of Egypt's, Shukairy found it necessary to justify his stand by explaining that it was not Fatah's terrorism that the P.L.O. objected to, but the timing of it which was not in accord with the P.L.O.'s plans and the orders of the Joint Arab Command. Afraid of losing out to Fatah in a power struggle, Shukairy obtained Nasser's permission to try to cajole Arafat into joining a united Palestinian front, but the Fatah leader refused since the time was ideal for Fatah to seize a dominant position among Palestinians. Arafat's readiness to defy Nasser focused a good deal of attention on the fact that only Fatah was willing to fight and take risks. Despite Fatah's meager military accomplishments, it emerged as an activist group and for most Arabs this was preferable to Ahmed Shukairy and the vapid rhetoric of the P.L.O.

Nasser was forced to find a way of wresting the limelight away from Arafat and Fatah. Toward the end of 1965 and in the beginning of 1966 signs of a new wave in Arab thinking began appearing with ever-increasing regularity in the Egyptian press. Articles discussing the possibility of a "preventive" war against Israel argued that h a measure was made necessary by Israel's imminent development of nuclear weapons. The leading advocate of this line of reasoning was Mohammed Hassanein Heykal, editor of the semi-official *Al Ahram* and Nasser's friend and adviser.

In the beginning of 1966, Arab leaders were convinced that Israel was on the verge of producing the atomic bomb. The Egyptian estimate was that Israel would have nuclear capability in two or three years, but Heykal was sure this achievement was even closer because Israel had been assisted by "many outstanding Jewish experts, especially Americans." In one of his widely read weekly columns, he wrote:

> The most significant factor today, which is a source of grave concern to the Arabs, is Israel's atomic potential and the need to be prepared for this potential.
>
> [Heykal revealed that the subject had been raised at two Arab summit meetings.] Arab life will not be possible in the shadow of Israel's atomic threat. The hopes of the Arab people will be precariously balanced on the edge of an awesome chasm for an indefinite period. This will give Israel the advantage of having no opponent and she will exploit this for the purpose of unlimited penetration and intervention.

Heykal argued that even if the Arabs were to manufacture their own atomic weapons, this would only create a balance of power, which in turn would deadlock the Palestinian problem and this is "precisely what Israel wanted" because once the Arabs possessed nuclear weapons, talks on regional demilitarization and disarmament would eventually take place and the territorial status quo would be maintained.

The debate over Israel's nuclear potential became another cause of inter-Arab divisiveness. Syria's Baath regime, always anxious to demonstrate its independence, took a different view. Unlike Egypt, Syria felt that the threat of Israel's nuclear potential would not change the Palestine issue and therefore was not a proper cause for embarking on a preventive war against the Jewish State. War, the Syrians argued, was in any event a necessity and must be pursued along conventional lines with the first stage being fedayeen activities.

The fear of Israel's atomic capability encouraged the view that time was on Israel's side and that rather than wait for the opportune moment, it was necessary to strike Israel before she actually obtained atomic weapons. As Egypt pressed to control the fedayeen movement by introducing a new propaganda tactic based on fear of Israel's atomic might, Syria continued supporting Fatah. The organization was a convenient means for the Baathist regime to show up Nasser as a temporizing, weak leader, unworthy to be the hero of Arab nationalism. The desire to play up Nasser's impotence in the matter of Palestine, rather than any respect for or belief in Fatah was the paramount motive for Syria's support of Fatah. Damascus' initial commitment to Fatah was not great. There was a considerable gap between her extremist slogans and actual military strength and Syria's military commanders knew they could not go too far in their struggle with Israel without the support of the Egyptian army. Even while provoking Nasser, the Baathists hoped Egypt would sign a mutual defense pact and join them in a program of sabotaging Israeli installations. Syria supplied Arafat with arms and a large variety of equipment for guerrilla warfare on condition that all actions be initiated from Jordan or Lebanon but not Syria.

But as Jordan and Lebanon increased their control over the terrorists and imposed restraints on Fatah, Syria had no choice but to permit the carrying out of some limited actions within her borders. These carefully controlled operations consisted of laying mines along the border and dirt roads leading to Israeli frontier settlements.

An army-led coup in February, 1966 brought an extremist faction of the Baath party to power and drastically altered the status of Fatah in Syria. The new ruling group's general orientation was pro-Peking. Soon the new Syrian strongmen set up their own Palestinian guerrilla units made up of men serving in the regular army. Fatah was considered an adjunct military force and for a time it seemed that it would be swallowed up by the Syrian army. The new Baathist regime demanded total obedience and even went so far as to imprison Arafat and other Fatah leaders for a short time on the pretext that they had carried out an unauthorized raid on Israel and had transferred arms from Lebanon to Syria without prior approval from the Syrian General Staff.

The Fatah heads resolved to free themselves from Syrian domination and moved the group's military command back to Beirut. The Baath party gave birth to a new Arab ideology proclaiming a "war of popular liberation" as the key to recovering Palestine. Damascus fancied itself the Hanoi of the Middle East and embarked on a program aimed at stirring the emotions of the entire population. The Algerian example and the success of guerrilla fighters elsewhere persuaded the Syrians that it was sufficient to label guerrilla actions a "war of liberation" and Israel a "foreign invader" to guarantee the successful outcome of their struggle. Damascus calculated that by comparing the Mideast conflict with the war in Vietnam the Arabs would gain the support of the Communist countries and the admiration of leftist movements throughout the world. Although Syria was aware of her military weakness, she believed Israel, like the U.S. in Vietnam, would not be able to contend with a protracted guerrilla war.

Syria's new provocative posturing soon exposed her to Israeli reprisals and she was no longer able to avoid blame for acts of sabotage as she had previously done with Fatah. The short-range border crossings by Syrian fedayeen elicited an Israeli response consisting of artillery bombardment and air strikes. In Damascus, the unsure new Baathist regime was thrown into a state of panic by Israeli retaliation. The Soviet Union was convinced that the "progressive" rulers of Syria were about to topple and decided to bolster the faltering regime and its war effort by maneuvering Egypt into taking military action against Israel.

Nasser, meanwhile, followed up his preventive-war-against-Israel propaganda with covert support for some fedayeen actions. In the summer of 1966 his relations with Hussein and the royal family in Saudi Arabia were seriously strained and the concept of Arab unity promoted by the summit conferences had done nothing to help the Egyptian president extricate his army from Yemen. Rejecting the guise of Arab solidarity as useless, Nasser ordered Egypt's operatives in Jordan and Saudi Arabia to intensify their subversive activities.

Abandoning the policy of not publicly supporting the fedayeen and responding to Ahmed Shukairy's call for direct action, Nasser gave the Palestine Liberation Organization permission to act against Israel from Jordanian bases. This was also in line with the Egyptian leader's tactic of infiltrating Jordan to weaken Hussein's regime. Once again the slogan, "the road to Tel Aviv is through Amman," was sounded and Shukairy was given the greatest latitude in propaganda claims in order not to lag behind Fatah.

Together Nasser and Shukairy exploited the vast propaganda apparatus at their disposal and whipped up a folk frenzy of hatred for Israel and belief in the fedayeen as the liberators of Palestine. Perhaps Nasser adopted this militant approach because he found the threat of retaliation from Israel to be less ominous than he had earlier expected. Indeed, until the summer of 1966 Israel's responses to fedayeen attacks were cautious. But what was restrained on Israel's part was interpreted by the Arabs as weakness. Egypt's behavior strengthened the position of Israel's hawks who demanded a strong blow against the Arabs before the latter began believing in their own strength. Although Israel knew that Syria stood behind Fatah's harassments, she avoided retaliating against Syria, choosing instead to strike at Jordan where the Fatah raids originated. Because of this, Nasser concluded that Soviet backing was the reason for Israel's failure to strike at Damascus instead of pro-Western Jordan.

On October 19, 1966 four P.L.O.-sponsored fedayeen infiltrated Israel from Lebanon. In a skirmish with an Israeli patrol three of the Arabs were killed and the fourth was taken prisoner. He told his captors that he and his comrades belonged to a new terrorist group called "Heroes of the Return." He said he had been recruited and trained by Shawfik el-Hut, head of the P.L.O. office in Lebanon. Nine days later a "Heroes of the Return" unit crossed over to Israel from Jordan and laid explosives near an Israeli border settlement in the Judean

Hills. Soon it was evident that internal competition was encouraging the formation of several terrorist groups. In one of the few relatively successful actions, one unit planted a mine on the tracks of Israel's railroad leading to Jerusalem. This time the explosive went off and wrecked a freight train. This attack was followed by a fedayeen ambush in which a civilian motorist was injured on the road to Jerusalem. The explosion of a delayed-timer device in a residential neighborhood of Jerusalem was credited by Shukairy in a radio broadcast to a newly organized fedayeen unit.

Ostensibly, the P.L.O. acted independently of Egypt, but, in fact, Nasser was not only supplying and guiding Shukairy, he was also maintaining contacts and giving arms to Fatah. It was at this time, in late 1966, that fedayeen began using Communist Chinese arms obtained through Damascus and Israeli intelligence later discovered that it was also during this period that a joint Egyptian-Syrian mutual defense pact had been arranged. The pact provided for coordination of Fatah activity between Syrian and Egyptian intelligence officers. It also called for Nasser to activate a fedayeen unit in Gaza where hitherto he had banned terrorist raids.

Tension in the Middle East mounted rapidly as Syria, with Russia's connivance, indulged in more widespread terrorist attacks on Israeli civilian installations. Syrian conventional military harassment was also stepped up. In the spring of 1967, events reached the first of several high marks of escalation that eventually led to the Six-Day War in June. In a major air battle, Israel shot down six Syrian, Soviet-made MIG's over the Golan Heights and chased others in hot pursuit almost to Damascus. A short time later, in May, a fedayeen was captured by Israel while carrying explosives and arms. He confessed to belonging to a group commissioned by the Syrian army to blow up several civilian targets in Israeli cities to terrorize the population on Israel Independence Day, May 15.

Soviet maneuvering prodded Egypt and spurred reckless fedayeen terrorism. Nasser and Israel were being drawn into a vortex of imminent war that neither wanted. The events of those days have been amply documented, but it is rarely recognized that the Palestinian fedayeen of today did not spring up in the aftermath of the crushing Arab defeat in the Six-Day War as is popularly supposed. On the contrary, Fatah, the P.L.O. and other fedayeen groupings were not a result of the June, 1967 war; they were a major factor in precipitating that conflict.

CHAPTER 5

Fedayeen in Action

*Following the Six-Day War, the Arabs in the ter*ritories captured by Israel remained relatively calm. The leaders of Fatah discussed and debated future plans to rouse the Arabs of the occupied zones to demonstrate to the forthcoming United Nations General Assembly that Israel was not in control in the territories and that war with Israel was, in effect, still going on. Two Arab conferences held in the summer of 1967 encouraged the fedayeen by revealing Arab intransigence on the question of negotiating a settlement with Israel. On August 28, 1967, the Arab summit conference opened in Khartoum, Sudan, and ended three days later with a resolution declaring Arab refusal to recognize the Jewish State, much less undertake negotiations with her. In the beginning of September, the Baath party conference was held in Damascus accompanied by the following declaration broadcast over Radio Damascus:

> By means of a fedayeen struggle we will retrieve Palestine and tear the Zionist settlement out by the roots. Fedayeen war will bring us to Tel Aviv today, and tomorrow to Haifa. Because of the fedayeen Israelis will swarm to the sea and airports to flee Israel.

Syria became the first Arab state to re-open its Army bases for fedayeen training. Two large bases near Damascus were put into operation—Al Hamma and Maisloun—especially for saboteurs. But at the same time, Syria avoided exposing herself as a fedayeen sponsor. Her assistance was strictly passive and did not permit fedayeen raids to be launched from her territory.

Algeria soon followed Syria's example and opened a training base for Palestinian youth. Algeria also sent cadres to train terrorists in Syria and agents to recruit Palestinian students in Europe for Fatah. Egypt also appeared as a patron of the new heroes of the Arab world because Nasser perceived that it might be unwise not to support the fedayeen at the very time they were the object of widespread affection among the Arab masses. Egypt was not persuaded that the fedayeen could effectively wage war against Israel, but it saw no harm in assisting the militants as part of an overall anti-Israel strategy. The Egyptians regarded the fedayeen as having both nuisance value insofar as Israel was concerned and also significance as a reminder to the world that the Arab-Israeli conflict included a humanitarian problem that could not be ignored: the homeless Palestinians.

Egypt's support of fedayeen terrorism as part of the political struggle against Israel did not expose Nasser to any great degree of danger since supplies and equipment were delivered to the fedayeen indirectly and no operations were launched from Egyptian soil. Some fedayeen units were trained in Egypt and members of Palestinian units in the Egyptian army were sent to Jordan and placed under the command of the Egyptian military attaché in Amman. Egyptian staff officers also set up an underground fedayeen organization in Israeli-occupied Gaza.

King Hussein of Jordan tried at first to prevent the establishment of guerrilla bases in his kingdom. He foresaw the dangers presented by the fedayeen, who, failing to operate inside Israeli-controlled land, would gather in Jordan's cities and press for his overthrow. The king wanted to avoid any entanglement with Israel over the fedayeen issue but he could not withstand the pressure of other Arab states and Jordan soon became the center of fedayeen activity.

Yasir Arafat arrived on the West Bank to execute Fatah's decision to transfer its military headquarters to occupied territory. He and his aides set up their first headquarters in Kfar Kabtiyah, a village near Nablus on the West Bank. But Arafat was impatient and instead of devoting his time to establishing bases and recruiting followers from among the local Arabs he pressed for immediate action. He also underestimated Israel's capability for deterring guerrilla war and these miscalculations were to prove fateful in Fatah's destiny.

On September 17, 1967, Fatah carried out its first post Six-Day War action by blowing up an irrigation pipe at Kibbutz Yad Hannah, which is located near the pre-June 1967 frontier. Two days later, as an attempted general strike by storekeepers on the West Bank failed, Fatah struck again. This time explosives were planted in a Jerusalem hotel and four people were injured. This incident was followed by sabotaging a kibbutz factory and a residence at a semi-cooperative farm. A sleeping three-year-old child was killed in the latter action.

Once again Fatah directed most of its raids against civilian targets. Restaurants, bus stations and open markets were popular sites for terrorist explosions. Explosives set in the huge Mahaneh Yehuda market in Jerusalem in December, 1968 killed twelve persons and injured several more. Both Fatah and the Popular Front for the Liberation of Palestine claimed credit. Fatah circulated a photo showing an automobile that the terrorist organization claimed had been loaded with explosives and parked near the market.

Holy places were also singled out for terrorist harassment and Jewish worshippers at several sites, including the Western Wall in Jerusalem, were ambushed and attacked with hand grenades. Political and religious considerations did not restrain the fedayeen who were also in the habit of shooting Katyusha rockets into Jerusalem, a city holy to Judaism, Christianity, and Islam.

In Europe, Fatah representatives soon joined Algerian envoys in enlisting followers among Palestinians enrolled at universities in West Germany, Austria, Spain, Italy and other countries. The prospective fedayeen were told that the Arab masses were waiting for their arrival as leaders to begin the popular uprising. Dozens of young Arabs, imbued with the idea of freeing their homeland, threw up their studies and flew to Algeria where they underwent short training courses in the use of arms and sabotage techniques. They were then sent to Lebanon and eventually from there to Syria and Jordan where they were given orders to infiltrate Israeli-occupied territories. Their task was made easier because of Israel's "open-bridges" policy allowing West Bank Arabs to cross and re-cross the Jordan at will to sell produce and visit relatives.

The students were café revolutionaries, armed with the theories of Mao Tse-tung and grandiose illusions about being welcomed by the local, oppressed populace. But most of them were strangers to the residents of the West Bank who turned out to be suspicious and hostile. The students were among the first of the Fatah members to be arrested by Israel and they told interrogators of their despair and bitter disappointment in not finding acceptance among their Palestinian brothers. Since most of them were ready to relinquish their roles as fighters, they were imprisoned by the Israeli authorities for a few months and then released and allowed to return to their studies abroad.

Arafat was joined in his attempts to mobilize Arabs living under Israeli administration by Dr. George Habash, a physician who had given up his practice to lead the leftist Popular Front for the Liberation of Palestine (PFLP). Habash appealed to the educated Palestinians, while Fatah relegated ideology to a secondary place and emphasized instead the liberation of Palestine and the dissolution of the Jewish State. Arafat and Habash's efforts were constantly thwarted by Israeli security agents who moved quickly after the Six-Day War to familiarize themselves with the occupied territories. They broke up newly organized cells, collected information from informers and kept in touch with the political mood of the population.

Arafat kept on the move, traveling to the different towns on the West Bank. Fatah wanted to set up regional commands to help organize Arabs on the West Bank and in the Gaza Strip into revolutionary cells in preparation for a popular uprising. The mukthars of various villages were approached and contacts were made with leading personalities of the West Bank. Commanders were named and a training course instituted, but the newly initiated Fatah activities came quickly to the attention of Israeli authorities and several Fatah and Popular Front activists were arrested. Arafat, known to his comrades as Abu Amar, was almost captured in one roundup. Israeli forces arrived at his hiding place in Ramallah but he escaped and hid in a Volkswagen parked nearby. A few days later Arafat left the West Bank and did not return.

The wave of arrests left the fedayeen without central leadership. Different bands of saboteurs attached themselves to villages, usually preferring to remain on the outskirts while receiving food and supplies from the resident farmers. Often caves were used as hiding places. In the towns, the PFLP tried to organize an underground among students and young intellectuals. The effort was largely unsuccessful because the PFLP operative was arrested along with several West Bank Arabs he had been in contact with. Among those detained by the Israelis were former Palestinian officers of the Egyptian, Iraqi and Syrian armies who had been ordered to volunteer for guerrilla action on Israeli territory.

The fedayeen operating from rural village bases were also eliminated by thorough-going Israeli patrols and security checks. Often the news that fedayeen were in the vicinity became common knowledge in the villages and subsequently became known to the Israeli authorities. Clandestine nests of fedayeen were cleared out and many guerrillas were captured while others were killed in clashes with Israeli troops. The winter of 1968 was one of unfulfilled hopes for those who thought it would be the first stage in the popular fedayeen war against Israel.

Fedayeen in Action

Faced with the difficulty of establishing bases in occupied territory, the fedayeen were forced to return to launching their attacks from neighboring Arab states. Bases to be used as both launching sites for raids and training camps were established by fedayeen groups all along the Jordanian border. These bases were used for short-range attacks that generally consisted of laying mines along roads and near civilian kibbutzim in the Jordan and Bet Shaan valleys. From bases near the Jordan River, fedayeen crossed over to the Arab towns of the West Bank. They would carry out a few operations and then hurry back to their sanctuaries on the East Bank of the Jordan. This became increasingly risky, however, as Israel intensified her watch along the vulnerable border.

Fences were constructed and army outlooks stationed along the Jordan River as a shield against fedayeen fording the river. Roving patrols also made it difficult for the fedayeen to penetrate very far into Israeli-held territory. Fedayeen casualty rates were inordinately high and their missions became suicidal. The infiltrators were relentlessly pursued and those who did get past the network of obstacles set up by the Israelis were run down by helicopter and mobile ground patrols.

Casualties were sustained by Israel as well and several senior officers were killed in hunting for fedayeen who had crossed the river forming a natural boundary between the occupied West Bank and Jordan. Israeli military leaders found they had to alter their tactics in order to limit losses. The daring frontal assault that had become the Israeli army's trademark was inappropriate in the new battle situation. Instead of advancing upon the enemy, the army was ordered to make use of its superior fire power and overwhelm the fedayeen with intensive barrages of automatic weapon fire. This method succeeded and the infiltrating marauders were decimated by the Israeli army. Intrusions from the East Bank were kept under control.

The more experience the Israeli troops gained in fighting the fedayeen, the more secure the border became. At first, fedayeen encountering Israeli forces were reluctant to surrender because they had been told during training that the Israeli army takes no prisoners. Fearing they would be killed anyway, many of the raiders put up a desperate and hopeless resistance. Israeli soldiers used loud speakers to urge the cornered enemy fighters to come forth and surrender. Those that did were brought before Israeli radio and television microphones to tell their fedayeen comrades that they had not been harmed once they surrendered. In 1969, a guerrilla spokesman conceded that the fedayeen casualty rate in West Bank incidents had reached ninety percent. Israeli army records show that from the Six-Day War through the end of 1969 actual fedayeen penetrations of Israeli-held territory decreased steadily and were only an ever-decreasing percentage of overall fedayeen anti-Israeli actions. On the Eastern Front, which includes Jordan, Lebanon, and Syria, Israel's success in driving the Palestinian saboteurs away from her borders is illustrated by the following statistics:

In the second half of 1967 a total of 115 fedayeen actions were carried out. Of these approximately fifty-three percent were infiltrations of up to three miles inside Israeli territory. In 1968 out of 922 actions, only thirty-three percent (monthly average) involved penetrating Israel's border defenses and in 1969, fedayeen attacks and incidents of harassment against Israel numbered over 2000, but only nineteen percent were penetrations.[1]

Nor were the long-range, across-the-border assaults particularly effective. Although the frequency of the firing had increased in the years since the Six-Day War, the number of Israeli casualties did not increase proportionally. From the conclusion of the Six-Day War until the end of 1967, the total number of fedayeen long-distance attacks on the Eastern Front amounted to 116 and Israeli casualties numbered forty-four dead and wounded. In 1968 the number of Fedayeen across-the-border barrages totaled 927 and Israeli casualties were 334. In 1969, the figure for hostile fedayeen actions of all kinds originating in Jordan, Lebanon and Syria rose to 2777 but Israeli casualties were only 354, only twenty more than the preceding year.

Israeli casualties, both civilian and military, resulting from fedayeen action totaled ninety-two dead and over 350 wounded from the Six-Day War to the end of 1968. Seventy-seven Israelis were killed by regular Arab forces, including forty-seven seamen who died in the sinking of the destroyer "Eilat" by Egypt. During the same period 768 fedayeen were killed, the majority members of Fatah.[2]

The largest fedayeen base in Jordan was Karameh in the Jordan Valley, north of the Dead Sea. Next to Karameh were 18,000 Jordanian villagers, but most of them fled eastward when the fedayeen settled in. In addition to Fatah, other fedayeen groups had built a cluster of smaller bases around the Karameh nucleus. Both operational and training bases were located in Karameh and it was the departure point for most fedayeen raids on Israel as well as the communications center for liaison with fedayeen operating on the West Bank.

The Israeli army was tempted by the strategic importance of Karameh to stage a retaliatory action there.

Only about 1000 of the villagers were still in the area—all men—and Israel regarded Karameh, situated only a few miles inside Jordanian territory, as a proper military target. On the 18th of March, 1968, an Israeli school bus traveling near the Jordanian border south of the Dead Sea in the area known as the *Arava* ran over a fedayeen mine. Two adults were killed and twenty-nine youngsters were injured. The incident was the straw that broke the camel's back as far as Israel was concerned. The decision was taken to wipe out Karameh, the source of intolerable terrorist harassment.

On March 21, at dawn, one of the most ambitious reprisals against the Palestinian fighters began with a column of Israeli armored vehicles moving across the Allenby bridge into Jordanian territory. In the lead were tanks, followed by half-tracks carrying paratroopers. Further north, some nineteen miles away, another Israeli force crossed the Damiyah Bridge into Jordan. A third unit consisting of airborne troops in helicopters was assigned rearguard action aimed at closing off approaches to Karameh while the other Israeli troops were in action. Their job was to isolate an area measuring thirty by six miles so that other units could move into Karameh and overwhelm the guerrilla bases.

One of the Israeli army's mistakes in the Karameh operation stemmed from engaging the enemy at several points outside of the main battle area. Afterwards, it was learned that most of Israel's casualties had occurred in the marginal zones and not in Karameh itself which had fallen fairly easily. Israel had imposed two major restraints on her forces: no unarmed civilians were to be harmed and clashes with the Jordanian army were to be avoided. It was this second prohibition that caused most of Israel's losses (twenty-nine dead, sixty-nine wounded).

Within the embattled area there were several Jordanian army posts and further eastward were four tank companies equipped with seventy U.S.-made Patton tanks. It was a serious error on Israel's part to assume that the Jordanian army would remain indifferent to an attack, even if it was not aimed at the army.

The Jordanians were astonished when the Israeli tanks began crossing the Allenby and Damiyah bridges. In Amman, King Hussein was awakened with the announcement that the Israeli army had invaded Jordan and was rapidly moving toward the capital. The King issued orders for Jordanian army troops to station themselves along the ridge next to the East Bank and to confront the invading troops there. In less than an hour, however, it was clear that the Israelis were not intending to attack Amman, but were concentrating on an area in the river valley. Israeli planes dropped leaflets saying that the troops intended to act only against the saboteurs in Karameh. Kol Yisrael, the Israel Radio Service, broadcast an announcement emphasizing that the move was only a police action and was not aimed at regular Jordanian troops or at penetrating deep into Jordanian territory. The Jordanian army subsequently opened an artillery barrage on the Israeli units, even though this was sure to bring an Israeli air strike to silence the cannons.

In Karameh, the reprisal was carried out according to plan. The unit assigned to enter the village was told to attack the fedayeen and take prisoner those who surrendered. The soldiers were instructed to keep an eye out for Abu Amar (Yasir Arafat) and his picture was distributed by unit commanders. But once again luck was with Arafat. Instead of remaining to fight, he and his closest aide escaped on motorcycles from Karameh to Es-Salt, 16 miles further eastward.

The Karameh action lasted most of the day as the Israeli forces combed surrounding guerrilla bases and the trenches for hiding fedayeen. Those that resisted were killed. Close to 200 fedayeen died in the action and 128 were taken prisoner. Forty Jordanian soldiers were killed. Israel had assumed that once the Jordanian army saw Israeli forces in broad daylight it would be deterred from attacking. But when the Israeli units entered the East Bank, the Jordanian troops opened up artillery fire and tanks in the area engaged Israeli armored in short exchanges. Israel's forces found themselves in a curious predicament—they were within range of Jordanian artillery and tanks but under orders not to advance. For hours they returned Jordanian fire while hardly moving at all. Israeli ground and armored units, trained to move rapidly and aggressively on the offensive, were forced into a stationary posture and consequently were at a disadvantage. The Jordanians were operating from fortified positions and had a distinct advantage. Israeli units taking part in the Karameh action spent twelve hours in enemy territory and were under artillery fire all that time.

In the wreckage of Karameh a large quantity of arms was found, including Soviet mortar launchers given to the fedayeen by Iraqi troops stationed in Jordan. The Jordanian armored units also suffered extensive damage resulting from Israeli air force strafing and rocket attacks. Four Israeli tanks and two armored carriers were damaged in the engagement and one of the burnt-out tanks was left in Jordanian territory where the fedayeen proudly displayed it in Amman along with the remains of the driver. One Israeli plane was downed but the pilot survived. All in all, Israel saw the Karameh attack as a success despite her considerable casualties.

Karameh marked a turning point in the post Six-Day

War guerrilla conflict of the fedayeen. Since March, 1968, the Palestinian guerrillas have built their bases a good distance from the border and the Jordan valley has become a no-man's land. Residents of the Arab border villages evacuated rather than be caught in the Israel-fedayeen crossfire. Although the Arab side of the fighting at Karameh was mainly carried on by the Jordanian army and most of the fedayeen fled or hid, Fatah created the myth that Karameh had been a great victory over the invading Israelis. The guerrillas described the incident as a "joint" battle in which they fought side by side with the Jordanian troops and prevented Israeli tanks from entering Amman.

The Arab victims of Karameh were buried with full honors accompanied by mass processions. Yasir Arafat was elevated to the status of hero despite the fact he had fled the besieged town and left his lower-ranking fedayeen comrades to their fate. Foreign correspondents were told by publicity-hungry Fatah functionaries that Karameh was the "Alamo" of the Palestinian Arabs and was the event that put an end to the legend of an invincible Israeli army. The propaganda worked and Fatah rose even further in the esteem of Arabs throughout the Middle East. The number of volunteers increased sharply and many Arabs were convinced that Karameh was the harbinger of a new era in the ongoing war against Israel, one that presaged ultimate victory for the Arabs.

Despite the optimism, fedayeen operations dampened somewhat after Karameh as Israeli patrols continued to keep the Jordan valley frontier sealed off and maintained a close watch on any attempt at fedayeen organizing among the Arabs in occupied lands. In the Gaza Strip the fedayeen had an easier time of it than their counterparts in the West Bank since the Egyptian army had left behind enormous quantities of war matériel while fleeing during the Six-Day War. Many residents of Gaza were trained in the use of arms as they had served in Palestinian units of the Egyptian army. Among them were former officers capable of leading fedayeen bands. The bitter frustration reigning in the Palestinian refugee camps in Gaza aided the fedayeen in recruiting young men. Even though Gaza is relatively small and the terrain open, the dense crowding of the camps provided the terrorists with cover and sanctuary and they were able to maintain a steady pace of terrorist attacks—many of them directed at Arabs suspected of cooperating with the Israeli authorities. Most of the anti-Israel actions were grenade attacks on Israeli vehicles.

Israel applied a policy of selective counter-punishment in Gaza. Individuals found collaborating with fedayeen were punished by the blowing up of their houses. This practice became one of the most controversial aspects of the Israeli occupation.

After Karameh, the fedayeen moved their headquarters and bases further inland, out of Israeli artillery range, to Es-Salt. The fedayeen felt safer here on the outskirts of a town of 30,000 residents. They established training camps and operational centers and roamed about freely, enjoying extra-territorial status. They were not, however, out of the reach of Israel's air force.

In April and May of 1968 the number of fedayeen incursions from Es-Salt dropped, but in June the number rose considerably and continued to spiral upward into July. In that one month forty fedayeen were killed in border incidents involving Arab guerrillas operating from Jordanian bases, principally Es-Salt. In July, Israel, despairing of Jordanian control over the fedayeen, struck the Es-Salt bases from the air.

Both the command headquarters of Fatah and the

Popular Front for the Liberation of Palestine shared the Es-Salt complex and it was hoped that Arafat would be found there, but he escaped unharmed. Other senior officers of Fatah were seriously injured and an estimated seventy fedayeen died in the air action. The Es-Salt strike was a heavy blow to the fedayeen. Their chief base had been devastated. Amid the smoke rising from burning buildings Israeli air force planes dropped circulars threatening "death to all who attempt to kill," and promising "life to all who are ready to live in peace!" Israel also carried out air attacks against the fedayeen bases in Syria. The destruction of major fedayeen concentrations caused the guerrillas to scatter their bases over a large area. The new camps were small and well-hidden sanctuaries. Operating from caves, wadis, and forests, the fedayeen had lost their proximity to the border and sustained heavy casualties while carrying out hopeless missions. Many died even before reaching the border. Their bases were no longer safe refuges; the long arm of Israel's air force became a nightmare.

Once the new bases were ferreted out by Israeli intelligence, the fedayeen began setting up some of their bases in Palestinian refugee camps in Jordan and Lebanon. By the winter of 1969, the United Nations Relief Works Agency, the organization responsible for administering the camps, admitted that the fedayeen were in control of the refugee centers in Jordan and Lebanon and dictated terms to the UNRWA officials. By settling in among the civilian refugees Israeli retaliation could be avoided since Israel would not attack the camps. The Popular Front for the Liberation of Palestine established its military headquarters in one of the suburbs of Amman and Fatah set up offices in the downtown area of the Jordanian capital.

The fedayeen began a campaign of pressuring the

Arab governments to supply them with anti-aircraft guns. They set up heavy machine guns to deter Israeli jets. At several points in southern Lebanon 20mm cannons were installed but these installations were soon spotted and knocked out of action by Israeli fliers. The air attacks were a severe psychological strain and several fedayeen commanders requested transfers for men whose nerves were frayed by the aerial reprisals.

Using mortars and rockets from afar represented a degeneration of the guerrilla war the fedayeen had declared against Israel. The main targets of the artillery bombardment were civilian settlements located near the border. The town of Bet Shaan in the Jordan Valley was shelled several times and a number of injuries and deaths occurred among the adults and children of that community. Another favorite target for Katuysha rockets was the Dead Sea Potash Works. Despite the often heavy Arab shellings no Israeli border settlements were abandoned. Instead the settlers spent many hours in underground shelters and at several kibbutzim, children were housed in bunkers. They grew accustomed to sleeping, eating, and studying while above them the piercing sounds of Katyusha rockets and mortars shattered the rural silence.

The fedayeen searched for a new combat approach. Having failed to achieve its objective from bases in Jordan, Fatah searched for a new proximity to Israel. The Syrian and Egyptian borders were effectively closed to the organization since both countries severely limited fedayeen operations on their soil. Yasir Arafat turned to Lebanon. Soon large numbers of fedayeen poured into the southwestern slopes of the Mt. Hermon range in southern Lebanon, an area offering favorable terrain and direct access to Israel. The idea was to first establish a network of Fatah bases and then begin operations. The

Popular Front gave up its attempts at guerrilla war and confined itself to underground activities. As a cover the Front used various established institutions such as the U.N.-sponsored Palestinian refugee occupational center in Ramallah that was used as a convenient place for distributing money to families of fedayeen who had been imprisoned. The profits of the center's cafeteria were expropriated by the PFLP for this purpose.

Israel's policy of allowing members of divided families to cross the Jordan to be reunited was exploited by the PFLP to infiltrate key fedayeen figures into Israeli-controlled territory. Women were the driving force in the Front's underground cells. Arab girls were assigned various tasks and served as decoys to protect saboteurs. The Front correctly assumed that Israel would be more lenient toward Arab women and thus it was that female fedayeen set the charges that blew up the supermarket in Jerusalem and the student cafeteria at the Hebrew University and carried out other terrorist acts.

The PFLP's jealousy of Fatah caused it to stage ever-bolder operations. It chose a highly visible and strategic target in the occupied Golan Heights—a section of the Anglo-American Petroleum Tapline which carries crude oil from Saudi Arabia via Jordan and Syria to Lebanon's Mediterranean coast. The Tapline brought huge profits to the Arab states and did not benefit Israel. Nevertheless, according to the Front's Maoist ideology, the Tapline was a proper guerrilla objective because it represented both Western imperialism and reactionary Arab regimes, namely Jordan and Saudi Arabia. The fact that Saudi Arabia subsidized Egypt and Jordan and the fedayeen organizations did not deter the Front which struck the pipeline in June, 1969, after infiltrating the heights from Lebanon. A sizable section of the pipe was blown up and the only harm to Israel was the temporary pollution of the Jordan River's waters from the leaking oil.

The second half of 1969 also brought an increase in terrorism on Israeli territory proper, i.e; the pre-1967 area of the Jewish State. In June, there were several incidents of sabotage in Jerusalem and pipelines leading to the Haifa oil refinery were blown up. There was also a spate of terrorist attempts in Tel Aviv and Katyusha rockets were fired into residential areas of Jerusalem. Activity on the Lebanese border also reflected a new fedayeen mood resulting from the Beirut government's failure of nerve in dealing with the Palestinians. From Mt. Hermon, the area that eventually came to be known as "Fatahland," infiltrators crossed into northern Israel and terrorized settlements.

Israel retaliated against Jordan by attacking irrigation canals of the U.S.-financed Ghor dam from the air and Fatah-infested villages inside Lebanon were cleansed of guerrillas. On January 1, 1970, the fedayeen accomplished their first kidnapping of an Israeli when they crossed the Lebanese border and seized Shmuel Rosenwasser, a watchman at a northern border farming settlement. They tried to exploit his kidnapping as a means of wresting political recognition from the Israeli government. Israel refused to negotiate directly with Fatah on the grounds that the International Red Cross did not recognize the fedayeen as official political entities. Rosenwasser was exchanged in the spring of 1971 for an imprisoned fedayeen. The intensified guerrilla campaign of 1969 and 1970 elicited determined counter measures by Israeli security forces who arrested several terrorists and again effectively disrupted their operations both inside Israel and in the occupied areas. Included among those arrested were indigenous Israeli Arabs operating in Haifa and elsewhere in northern Israel. This group had been recruited by Arabs from the West Bank and received arms and explosives from Lebanon via the sea. Among its leaders was a bedouin sergeant in the Israeli army who aided the saboteurs to elude capture by Israeli forces. The head of the group was an Arab from Acre, on the Mediterranean coast near Haifa, who was married to a Jewish woman. In the period of a few months more than 600 saboteurs and suspected fedayeen collaborators were rounded up in the territories. By the fourth anniversary of the Six-Day War a general accounting of fedayeen action showed meager results in the territories.

Fedayeen losses for the June, 1967-January 1, 1971, period totaled 1828. Fatah lost the most men, 938 followed by the Popular Front for the Liberation of Palestine, 147. Popular Liberation Forces lost 134 and the Syrian-sponsored Saiqah 133; other groups lost 122 and unidentified fedayeen deaths amounted to 354. The heaviest losses were in the Jordan area. These figures were provided by Israeli intelligence and are based on actual body counts and a study of fedayeen death announcements.

Arabs living under Israeli occupation suffered greatly from fedayeen violence. Figures available for 1969 and 1970 show that in 1969 thirteen Arab residents of the West Bank and eighteen in Gaza were killed in fedayeen actions. Sixty-two West Bank Arabs and 309 in Gaza were wounded during the same period. In 1970 fedayeen-caused deaths among Arabs of the West Bank numbered five while in Gaza forty were killed. The number of wounded in the West Bank were sixty-seven and 684 in Gaza where the casualty rate has remained high.

In comparison with the total number of Israeli deaths—748—civilian and military, resulting from both regular and irregular armed hostilities from June, 1967 to January, 1971, the fedayeen suffered more than twice the losses of their enemy. The fedayeen only caused less than half the Israeli deaths. Considering that they gained no territory and sustained a high casualty rate, the futility of the fedayeen struggle against Israel is apparent.

NOTES

1. Figures do not include artillery attacks by regular armed forces of Arab states.
2. Official Israeli figures based on body counts and fedayeen publications.

CHAPTER 6

Pursuit in the Desert

*The Judean Wilderness is a fantastic lunar land-*scape of sharp cliffs, twisting wadis (dry river beds), and convoluted hills broiling under a relentless sun during the day and turning unexpectedly cold at night. There is no water available, and without expert guides hikers can easily lose their way and perish. This is the area where Bishop Pike lost his life. It is here that bands of Arab terrorists try to infiltrate into Israel and the towns of the West Bank. They are stopped by the desert patrols of the Israeli Army, who know every cave and every footpath through the desert.

The patrols regularly organize saboteur hunts

through the desert in which infiltrators are apprehended and often killed. Usually the pursuit takes the patrol across steep cliffs and caves in over 100-degree temperature.

A typical patrol begins with the soldiers standing around in small groups, their weapons in their hands. The officers huddle over a map, immersed in consultations and plans for the pursuit. Close by, the field radios are humming. Earlier it had been discovered that a group of saboteurs had crossed the frontier under cover of darkness and had continued westward, deep into the heart of Israeli territory.

The officers debate how far the saboteurs had been able to go, their possible directions and the routes they might have chosen and, most important, the best place to trap them. It is clear to them that everything has to be done to prevent the saboteurs from reaching the Arab population centers where they could find cover, organize their operations and pinpoint targets for attack. In this pursuit, as in previous ones, the patrols combing the Jordan Valley and the Judean Desert would be protecting civilian targets in Jerusalem and its environs.

The men prepare for the pursuit as if it is going to be a decisive battle. When the area commander arrives and is briefed by the field officers, the hunt for the fedayeen begins.

The doctor accompanying the Israeli patrol—a captain—checks the first-aid packs which he and his assistant carry on their backs.

It is early morning. The sun is already beating down strongly. Mists rise up from the Dead Sea, reducing visibility. The officers decide on the least likely direction: southeast, toward the high cliffs of the Judean Desert. In their estimation, the saboteurs intended to cross the

Judean Wilderness in the direction of the hills around Hebron and not toward Jerusalem. This was an area in which no pursuit after saboteurs had yet taken place. Before they set out someone remarks: "This will be a sweep through the lowest place in the world." The area is 1290 feet below sea level.

The sun rises higher in the sky as the patrol crosses mountains and canyons. There are no laws in a chase like this. No pursuit is like the last one. Each one requires different tactics.

There are standard rules for traveling in this wilderness and there are safety precautions that must be taken, but one can never tell what the infiltrators will do. Those with lots of physical stamina can cover huge distances in one night. Others disregard the rules of the game and are willing to take the risk of marching even in daylight. There are those who fight fiercely, almost suicidally, because they have been fed the stories that the Israelis never take prisoners. Others are willing to surrender even before they've been called on to do so, although they still have ample stores of arms and ammunition at hand.

The patrol moves deeper into the desert area, moving at first on the crests of cliffs and then into an area of dusty hills between open plains without a bit of shade. Around noon the route takes a sharp turn to the east, toward the rocky canyons of the Qumran region. This is the wilderness that sheltered the Essenes and other rebels against ancient Greece and Rome, a land honeycombed with the caves that housed for centuries the ancient scrolls of the wilderness sects. The cliffs towering above the gloomy canyons are terrifying. The saboteurs could have found cover here in a cave or behind a rock. At any moment the pursuers might be fired upon.

"This is a real tough gang," one of the scouts

says, checking on a map the route the saboteurs have taken. They managed to penetrate to a great depth. Usually, groups of infiltrators cannot get very far during the first night. After that they seek cover during the daylight hours. Most of the bands are caught in this area. Few of them get much further. This bunch must have had considerable stamina. A glance at the twisted route they took indicates that they had already traveled thirteen miles up steep cliffs and hills. The question is, how will they stand up during the next few hours, in the oppressive heat, without water? Thirst is a crucial factor in the desert.

The Israeli officers take pains to ensure the provision of water for desert patrols. Both the Judean Desert and the Jordan Valley lie under a fierce blanket of heat that often reaches 113 degrees. The loss of body fluids during a pursuit is so great there is real danger of dehydration. The heat generally begins to take its toll quickly. Then men become exhausted and their reactions slow down drastically.

Everything possible is done to keep the men on pursuits supplied with cold drinking water. Filled canteens are placed in containers packed with ice, and delivered to the desert patrols by jeep, wherever possible. For the most part, however, jeeps cannot get to the places where the patrols are operating, and helicopters take over the vital task of delivering water.

The desert chase has become a specialized skill in which Israeli units excel. The fedayeen, too, have gained experience from these pursuits, but most of the infiltrators are killed or caught, and very few manage to return to their bases to teach their comrades the lessons they have learned.

The patrol enters a deep wadi. There is a good chance the saboteurs might be hiding in some of the caves dotting the high cliffs. Fedayeen usually hide out in caves and open sudden fire from there. Two soldiers walk slowly along the sloping banks, each watching for caves on the other side.

Suddenly there is a shout from the slope: "Cave above you! Twenty meters!" Somebody off at the side opens up with machine gun fire directly into the mouth of the cave. A second soldier approaches and fires into the cave with a submachine gun. A "cleanup squad" edges its way inside and checks to see if there is anyone in the cave. From the flanks and from above they are covered by others. The soldiers work quickly. Someone shouts: "Move your ass, where do you think you're strolling—on the seashore?" And another voice: "Watch out for that dirty area!" The reference is to a small cleft, choked with high rocks and some bushes, near the entrance of a cave.

The patrol moves forward, the helicopters "jumping" the soldiers to the next wadi and returning for more. As always, the helicopters are an essential part of the pursuit. They save time and strength by flying the soldiers into canyons difficult to reach on foot.

At three o'clock in the afternoon there is still a chance the infiltrators will be caught before nightfall. The pursuers are tense, but everything is moving along well.

The unit reaches the top of a hill that commands the intersection of some deep canyons. Half a mile away there is a cliff with two small openings into caves. The patrol commander looks across the canyon at the caves. Suddenly he turns to another officer and says, "They must be there. In the caves on that cliff!"

He is going by intuition. A unit armed with machine guns is positioned opposite the cliff, about five hundred yards away. They open with heavy fire into the opening of the cave; chips of rocks fly off in all directions. Other forces flank the cliff from left and right.

The firing continues. Suddenly a piece of white cloth is seen in the entrance of the cave. The machine guns stop firing. A barefoot saboteur bursts out of the cave waving his white undershirt as a sign of surrender. A few moments later two more saboteurs emerge from the cave and after them another three. The six Arabs climb up the cliff with their hands raised. At the top, stand soldiers with their weapons pointed at the band of infiltrators.

Two of the fedayeen are trembling. They think they will be killed. Some of the soldiers blindfold them and begin a preliminary interrogation. Only one of the infiltrators is stubborn and refuses to answer questions. The oldest of the saboteurs mumbles his story.

He says he is from Khan Yunis in the Gaza Strip and had simply been asked to serve as a guide. Aside from that he knows nothing. Later, his Kalatchnikov rifle is found in the cave. The others are originally from Hebron and one from Jerusalem. They say they were heading for Hebron and planned to attack civilian transport.

The interrogation is conducted with the saboteurs lying on the ground. In the meantime the other Israeli soldiers join the interrogators. There is no sign of hatred. No one beats the prisoners, and no one thinks of torturing them. It is all very businesslike. The feeling that seems to dominate the patrol is one of contentment that the pursuit is ended without casualties and without bloodshed.

A few soldiers approach the cave. One calls out to anyone still inside and another tosses in two hand grenades. When the dust settles they enter the cave and find guns, hand grenades, and a good deal of other equipment. The water canteens are empty. At the side is a large transistorized radio receiver the saboteurs carried with them, cigarettes, and a woolen hat.

The fedayeen are to be brought in for interrogation. Their eyes are blindfolded with their own shirts. Before they set out on the way back the boots they abandoned in the cave are returned to them. The patrol commander radios back to his home base: "The operation is completed. We've got six live ones."

CHAPTER 7

Fedayeen Kaleidoscope

Although the name Fatah is synonymous with the Palestinian guerrilla movement in the minds of many Western readers and is often used as a generic term for all fedayeen, it is only one of several Palestinian guerrilla and terrorist organizations.

The large number of fedayeen groups and splinter factions reflects a divisiveness that has always plagued the Arab world. Bitter factionalism, ideological disputes, and personal rivalries divide the various Palestinian groups and one of the chief reasons for Arab failures in conflicts with Israel has been the lack of coordination and solidarity.

Fedayeen Kaleidoscope

The Palestinians and the fedayeen have long suffered from disastrous internal squabbling. Even before Israel came into being in 1948, the Arab community in Palestine could not effect a coalition and in later years, after the Six-Day War, the fedayeen repeated the pattern of fragmentation.

Many fedayeen groups spring up suddenly, are active for a short time and then disappear. Arab sources concede that more than sixty fedayeen organizations have emerged on the Mideast scene in recent years in this capricious manner. Some estimates indicate that there have been as many as 100 groups defining themselves as fedayeen dedicated to the liberation of their Palestine. Despite their single-minded goal, the destruction of the state of Israel, the fedayeen have also not accomplished overall coordination. Such efforts to foster unity as the creation of the Palestine Liberation Organization, a Fatah-dominated umbrella organization, have failed to gain the affiliation of all fedayeen. The Popular Front for the Liberation of Palestine, one of the best-known fedayeen groups, refuses to join the P.L.O. and the Popular Democratic Front for the Liberation of Palestine withdrew from the P.L.O. after a dispute concerning information policies. In Jordan, attempts to unify the embattled fedayeen in their struggle against King Hussein's forces under the jurisdiction of the combat arm of the P.L.O., the Palestine Armed Struggle Command's Central Committee, were unsuccessful.

Ideological differences account in part for the fragmentation of the Palestinians, but the desire of various people to enhance their reputations is the usual reason for a new fedayeen grouping coming into existence. Personal rivalries and greed contribute to the multiplication of guerrilla or "commando" (as they prefer to be known because of the connotation of a disciplined, non-terrorist combat unit) groups.

Arab documents indicate that the creation of a fedayeen force can sometimes be nothing more than an act of spite by an embittered man. One such example is contained in a letter sent by the Criminal Investigation Department of the Lebanese headquarters of the Arab Liberation Front to the organization's Secretary General. The letter was found during the Israeli army's sweep of "Fatahland" in May, 1970. Dated September 21, 1969, it describes a former member of the Popular Front for the Liberation of Palestine—General Command—who was expelled for "immoral behavior" and who then set up his own fedayeen band called "The Front for the Rescue of Palestine." Following is a translation from the Arabic of the captured document:

From Arab Liberation Front
Central Headquarters
Criminal Investigation Unit
To: The Secretary General
Subject: The Front for the Rescue of Palestine

The founder of the Front for the Rescue of Palestine, a person named Abed Al-Hatib, now at the Ein Al-Halua camp in Lebanon, is a Palestinian from Ras Al Ahmed and was a *mulazem* [lieutenant] in the Popular Front—General Command. He was responsible for the military and political organization of the Front in southern Lebanon. The above-mentioned gave parties for a member of Lebanese intelligence in his house in Al-Halua. He bought a Peugeot automobile with Front funds and began wasting money. Among other deeds, he served Lebanese intelligence and the Popular Front [General Command] was forced to discharge him.

Following this he founded an organization called "The Front for the Rescue of Palestine."

Hatam Fuhud, who is thought to be one of the ranking members of Lebanese intelligence, helped prepare the groundwork. Both Al-Hatib and Fuhud succeeded in attracting members from other groups by luring them with money. Girls were exploited to collect money. Such was the case of Saad and Fatma Ria, Palestinians from Lebanon who collected money in the name of Al Fatah, the Popular Front and the Palestine Liberation Front totaling 75,500 Lebanese lira [approximately $20,385] in one month. The money was used for patronizing night clubs in Beirut. Receipts bore the stamps of several Front organizations. The Lebanese government was in collaboration with Al-Hatib in order to hurt the reputation of the fedayeen. The government, however, finally arrested Al-Hatib as if to show that it is really concerned with the good name of the fedayeen movement. This was reported in the Lebanese press under the headline: "Lebanese Authorities Arrest Band of Swindlers Guilty of Extorting Money from Citizens in the Name of the Fedayeen."

Other documents taken during the Fatahland operation reveal that discord among the fedayeen was aggravated by problems of morals and discipline. Several papers are correspondence and orders involving charges of dereliction of duty, murder, theft, drunkenness, desertion, and homosexuality. One document is a lengthy record of a hearing convened in April, 1969, by the Arab Liberation Front, a group set up and financed by the

Baath party of Iraq, into charges of overt homosexual behavior by the deputy commander of one of the Front's camps in Lebanon. The testimony of the witnesses describes the seduction of a low-ranking recruit. The Deputy Commander, known by the *nom de guerre*, Ahmed Abdullah, confessed his guilt and blamed it on the devil who "misled him." Ahmed Abdullah was expelled from the Arab Liberation Front for his misdeeds.

One of the most telling documents captured is a general report compiled by one of the Arab Liberation Front's officers after a visit to one of the organization's camps in Lebanon. The report is addressed to the Front's commander of the Lebanese region and is dated July 22, 1969.

"One of the things I noticed," the officer, Abud Alfarhi, writes, "in this camp [17th of July Base] is the general mood of defeatism and the larger number of men who desert the base. The reason for this is the attitude of the base's officers. The commander is Lieutenant Hamad Abdullah, a man lacking the proper attributes. An additional reason is the presence of mercenary elements who joined the Front from other fedayeen groups and who try with all their might in deceptive ways to harm the Front and in this way to make their former organizations look good. They do this by spoiling the moral aspect of the Front. . . . A third reason is the presence of hired elements who are only interested in receiving salaries and are uninterested in any revolutionary goals or the reality of the Arab people and the Palestine problem."

Alfarhi goes on to discuss "lazy" fedayeen at the base and the lack of revolutionary principles among the camp's officers. He recommends that the overall commander for Lebanon take over supervision of the base in question and rectify conditions there by "instituting the proper political and revolutionary ideas and spirit."

The malaise of futility and jealous attempts by one fedayeen group to compromise another because of ideological or personal reasons has been evident throughout the fedayeen movement. The Arab countries have added to the confusion and internecine warfare by exploiting the Palestinian issue for political purposes and exerting control over new fedayeen organizations.

Egypt dominated the Palestine Liberation Organization, which was created by Arab summit conferences prior to the Six-Day War. Ahmed Shukairy headed the P.L.O. and the Palestine Liberation Army, which consisted of Palestinian units within the framework of the Egyptian, Syrian, and Iraqi regular armies. Following the Six-Day War, Shukairy's decline in prestige enabled Yasir Arafat to take over—with Egypt's approval—the remaining fragments of the Palestine Liberation Organization, including its propaganda offices in Europe and the United States. Shukairy retired to obscurity in Beirut.

After June, 1967, the Palestine Liberation Army was reformed to include a fedayeen force called the Popular Liberation Forces. The Palestine Liberation Army still exists and several of its units are stationed with Egyptian troops at the Suez Canal. One Palestinian unit of the pre-1967 P.L.A. was moved to Jordan and attempted to carry out fedayeen missions as part of the Popular Liberation Forces. The pre-1967 Palestinian contingent of the Iraqi army was also stationed in Jordan and many of its members have been absorbed into the Iraqi-sponsored Arab Liberation Front. The Syrian unit of the old P.L.A. became the nucleus of the Baath-supported fedayeen group, As-Saiqah.

Arafat took steps to insure Fatah's hegemony over the other fedayeen. The Palestine Liberation organization came under Fatah's domination by means of the formation of a Palestinian National Council. Fatah has forty representatives out of a total of 115 and Arafat serves as president of a ruling executive council. Arafat is invited to attend high-level inter-Arab meetings and the offices of the P.L.O. abroad stress Fatah in their publications and propaganda. However, if pressed, as Saadat Hassan, the P.L.O. representative in New York has been in interviews, the P.L.O. spokesmen abroad insist they represent "all fedayeen."

They do not, however, represent Fatah's chief rival, the leftist Popular Front for the Liberation of Palestine, which boycotts the P.L.O. The PFLP's leader, Dr. George Habash, advocated a joint front incorporating all fedayeen organizations on equal footing. Arafat insisted on representation based on a group's number of members. Through the structure of the P.L.O. and by means of financial subsidies paid by the oil-rich Arab countries of Saudi Arabia, Kuwait, and the Sheikdoms of the Persian Gulf but administered by Cairo, Egypt was able to control Fatah until Nasser's death in September, 1970.

Syria's bid for dominance over the fedayeen was first expressed in her early support for Fatah. Subsequently the Syrian Baathists set up their own Saiqah organization. The movement is financed and equipped by Damascus with Syrian army issue and its members train in Syrian army camps. Ideologically Saiqah supports the idea of a Palestinian state but stresses the Baath concept of pan-Arabism. Operations are directed by the Syrian general staff and the group is used to suit Syrian political aims such as infiltrating Lebanon.

The Iraqi Baathists, not to be outdone by their rivals in Damascus, also set up a fedayeen force—the previously mentioned Arab Liberation Front. This group, consisting of no more than one hundred fighting men, has not been particularly active and appears to exist for propaganda and prestige purposes only. It has units stationed in Jordan but chose to keep out of the fighting between the Jordanian army and the fedayeen. The Arab Liberation Front emphasizes the overall Arab struggle against Israel rather than the Palestinian national claims specifically.

Even Jordan, which has engaged the fedayeen on her territory in armed battle, has attempted to set up her own fedayeen unit which would take orders from King Hussein. Called the Front of National Sacrifice, it came into existence after the Six-Day War and was commanded by Hussein's uncle, Sharif Nasser Ben Gamil. It carried out a few actions against Israel but was disbanded after a few months.

The Communists in Jordan, Lebanon, and Iraq decided that they too should adopt the fedayeen fashion and in March, 1970, the Arab Communist parties established their fedayeen group known as Forces of the Partisans. It is not a member of the P.L.O., and, in contrast to the other fedayeen groups, supports the Soviet Union's Mideast policies which are ambivalent on the question of the Palestinian entity.

Few of the fedayeen organizations possessing spirited, patriotic names do much actual fighting. Even many of the groups federated under the Palestine Armed Struggle Command limit their military activity to occasional, sporadic and futile actions. One area of intense activity is the war of words and it is here that much fedayeen bad feeling has been generated as various groups strive to outdo each other in claiming fictitious and grandiose victories over Israel.

There is not one significant fedayeen organization that has not undergone purges, ideological disputes, and splintering. At the same time there is a reverse process by which small units of fedayeen will join a larger conglomeration, usually Fatah, in return for prestigious positions for the leaders and other forms of patronage.

George Habash's Popular Front for the Liberation of Palestine is a prime example of a militant Palestinian organization that has experienced several mergers and splits. Habash is an intense, handsome, middle-aged physician who was born in Palestine and who reportedly engaged in guerrilla and terrorist activities at the time of the 1948 Arab-Israeli war. He later founded a political party in Lebanon—*ei Haraka al Caumiyyin Arab* (Movement of Arab Nationalists)—which for many years was a pro-Nasser movement committed to the concept of Arab unity. Its slogan was "Unity, Liberation, Revenge." The party was in close contact with Egyptian intelligence and its publications were financed by the Egyptians. But by the time of the Six-Day War Habash's party had abandoned its belief in Nasser's ability to unite the Arabs, which according to Habash's thinking is a necessary step before Palestine can be liberated. A Marxist ideology replaced Nasserism as the party's political line. After the Six-Day War, Habash decided to set up his own fedayeen force. In November, 1967, Habash's Popular Front for the Liberation of Palestine came into being by the amalgamation of two groups formerly affiliated with the Arab Nationalist Movement—Heroes of the Return and The Youth of Vengeance—and a third group, the Palestine Liberation Front, headed by a former Syrian army officer named Ahmed Jibril.

Within eight months the coalition splintered over personal disagreements and the question of loyalty to Nasser and Ahmed Jibril set up his own small group called the Popular Front for the Liberation of Palestine-General Command. The PFLP-GC gained notoriety for two terrorist actions—planting a bomb aboard an Israel-bound Swissair jet that exploded and caused the death of crew and passengers and the ambush of an Israeli school bus along the Lebanese border in the spring of 1970. Jibril's organization is credited with a fairly high level of military competence. It is based in Syria.

In mid-1969 another former Habash disciple, Ahmed Zahrur, broke away from Jibril to form the Arab Movement for the Liberation of Palestine. Habash regrouped his followers but suffered another, potentially more significant, defection when an extreme leftist faction led by a 35-year-old Jordanian Christian named Naif Hawatmeh severed its connection with the PFLP and formed the Popular Democratic Front for the Liberation of Palestine. Hawatmeh, a rigorous Maoist, accused Habash of being a "petty bourgeois, a fascist, and a demagogue." The sharp differences between Habash and Hawatmeh's followers have led to shooting on some occasions.

After Fatah and Habash's PFLP, the most significant fedayeen groups are the Syrian Saiqah and Popular Liberation Forces of the Palestine Liberation Organization. The remainder of the fedayeen groupings have small memberships and are relatively inactive militarily.

On the occupied West Bank fedayeen activity is carried out principally by Fatah and the PFLP. The latter has gained adherents among the intellectual class. Saiqah is also represented to a limited extent. In Gaza the chief fedayeen antagonists are Fatah, Popular Liberation Forces and the PFLP. In Jordan most of the fedayeen maintained camps, while in Lebanon Fatah and Saiqah are dominant.

The members of the Popular Liberation Forces, who number, according to the season approximately 800 fighters, enjoy the best conditions of all the fedayeen. They receive higher wages than members of Fatah, but the latter enjoy the prestige of belonging to the foremost fedayeen force. Outstanding fedayeen in Fatah receive cash bonuses. The PFLP pays its members a small monthly allowance but, the PDFLP, poorest of the fedayeen, says its members receive no wages and receive only food, clothing, and lodging.

With the exception of the largest fedayeen groups, there is little of substance differentiating most of the organizations. Although ideological differences play a role in the rivalries among Fatah, the PFLP and the PDFLP, most fedayeen formations are separated by minor conflicts based on personality disputes and opportunism. Often an argument with an officer or the prospect of earning more is enough to induce a fedayeen to leave one group and join another.

Fatah pitches its appeal in terms of *jihad*, Islamic holy war, and in this way appeals to the lowest common denominator of the Arab masses. Because of Arafat's earlier connection with the Moslem Brotherhood and his religious orientation, Fatah has attracted Arab Palestinian nationalists and Moslem activists who are *not* enthusiastic about leftist ideologies and beliefs.

Habash, a Christian graduate of the American University in Beirut, has had success in appealing to Palestinian intellectuals and elitists who favor his revolutionary doctrine and who are intrigued by his intellectual-turned-man-of-action stance. While Fatah confines its fighting to the Mideast, Habash's PFLP has gained world fame by the bold hijackings of international jet liners. Habash is determined to wage his war everywhere but in areas under Israeli control. He has failed to mount the type of military offensive Fatah has achieved and has consequently fashioned a philosophy borne of his organization's failure to take root in the occupied territories. In sensational and dramatic newspaper and magazine interviews, Habash stresses the value of a plane hijacking or the bombing of a Jewish store or Israeli airlines office abroad as a means of riveting world attention on the Palestinian cause. In sharp contrast to the unlikely figure of paunchy Yasir Arafat, Habash is an upper-class Palestinian, an educated professional. He exerts personal appeal and the Front's flamboyant deeds have created a guerrilla theater of Palestinian resistance in which hundreds of uninvolved bystanders are endangered. His good looks and magnetism have attracted several educated girls to his movement.

Radical youth of America and Europe have been delighted with the exploits of such daredevil PFLP performers as Leila Khaled, the dark, slim, striking-looking 28-year-old Palestinian girl who hijacked a TWA jet to Damascus in the summer of 1969 and unsuccessfully attempted the same thing with an El Al jet a year later. Pictures of Leila wearing Arab guerrilla headdress and looking pensively at a submachine gun cradled in her arms compete for space with "Che" posters in the comfortable apartments of Beirut intellectuals and in such modish pro-fedayeen publications as the Paris magazine, *Jeune Afrique*. The participation of girls in the front's operations has deeply impressed the *macho*-oriented mentalities of many simple Arabs.

One of the avowed aims of The Popular Front for the Liberation of Palestine is the liberation of Arab society from "male chauvinism" at the same time that it liberates Palestine from Israel. It attacks "the governing reactionary cultures and rotten habits, the cultures and habits of religion, tribal, feudalist ideas which insist . . . on enclosing a woman . . . to restrict and isolate her."

Mona Saudi, a 25-year-old PFLP activist, says, "the presence of any woman in society was a sexual presence; now she's becoming a human being equal to man."

A PFLP ideologist says, "Girls in slacks running around on Hamra [Beirut's chic shopping and café district] imitating Hollywood film styles and without real political education have a false freedom like the freedom of girls in short skirts and cosmetics in Hong Kong. . . . They continue [to be] slaves; the difference is they were less sophisticated before."

The PFLP's solution is "to destroy and rebuild a revolutionary society." Leila Khaled says women must fight two battles: one against Zionism and Israel and the other "against man and the ideas that he practices on the woman. At the same time that she meets the enemy she frees herself."

Although even the traditionally minded Fatah has set up training courses for women, most of the fediyat (feminine plural of fedayeen) in Fatah are recruited to collect money, care for children, and administer first aid.

In the PFLP Leila Khaled and Mona Saudi have found an outlet for their activist natures. Generally, the women guerrillas are less likely to yield to interrogation when captured and display considerable personal courage and dedication. The fediyat are exceptional among Arab women for they have broken with family traditions and have overcome parental and social obstacles against female self-assertion.

Mona Saudi recalls that her family life in Jordan was stifling:

> If I wanted to go for a walk or stay late at the library, I couldn't. . . . In Amman *no* girl can go out

> alone at dark. . . . To meet the opposite sex is completely forbidden. . . .
> My brothers could go and come any time. They didn't have to do work at home. If I were sitting in a room with one of my brothers, he could ask me to get him a glass of water and I would be expected to do it. But I know I could never ask him to.
> If I did what my father—who is a very religious man and who is seventy-five years old, fifty years older than me—wanted, I wouldn't have finished secondary school, college, left home, or traveled. The most my father would have imagined for me was to be a teacher going to school in the morning, coming home at night, and waiting to get married.

Mona speaks of her father resentfully though respectfully while she refers to her mother lovingly—attitudes to be expected of a Western-educated girl kept in a sexually segregated and puritanical society with a double standard for male and female behavior. Mona's mother was married at twelve.

Mona went to Paris at eighteen without parental permission to study art. Today Mona is independent by any standard. Dressed in a baggy, brown sweater and slacks and with short, unkempt, light brown hair tumbling over horn-rimmed glasses, Mona is often seen in Beirut's Hamra Street cafés at night when few females go out unescorted.

Mona, who was jailed one month in 1970 in Copenhagen for plotting to assassinate former Israeli Premier David Ben Gurion, considers her life as an Arab woman "extraordinary." "In the whole society it is not accepted." She says that Palestine Liberation is easing the way out of their father's house for many girls. "Any ordinary case can be liberated by the revolution. . . . Any family would let a daughter go out for the reason of revolution but would not for any other reason. . . . Now if a father hears a radio broadcast about Leila Khaled, he might say to his daughter, 'You couldn't do like Leila.' But the daughter will reply, 'Yes, I can but you don't let me.' "

Even girls escaping male domination in their families still find themselves in guerrilla groups struggling to be free from male chauvinism. Mona Saudi says, "In the beginning of the Palestine Revolution men would refuse women's participation in man's work more out of politeness. Men considered women weak and their responsibility."

Dr. Nabilah Budny, a Palestinian-American doctor who has worked with the fedayeen explains, "There used to be a problem of even getting together in the same room. . . . It's hard for men to accept women participating in life of a camp—a mixed life. There is a feeling that you can't have relations with women out of marriage. But this happens normally. First there were separate camps for training but all came together for meetings. . . . There is still a very puritanical relationship between men and women although they in fact slept in the same room the fourteen days of the Jordan crisis [September, 1970]. But when it comes to sexual relations you have to be married or something like that."

Leila Khaled concedes that she didn't break every tradition in her life as an Arab woman. "A girl in Paris goes maybe every night to any apartment with a friend. In Beirut I can't do it," Leila says. "First of all, I can't accept that. I didn't grow up that way. . . . I haven't changed my traditions." She explains that "society would accept" if "I went on a mission with a man" but in "my daily life I can't do that. In daily life, if they see me going every day in Hamra Street or Rouche [Beirut's entertainment districts] with a man—not a relative on my arm, they won't accept it."

Leila, who maintains she was born in Haifa, said she "gave up everything—all social life" to prepare for her sabotage missions and never imagined that she would "get married through the revolution." "But through experiences and sharing in armed struggle, I changed my mind. It's unscientific to say 'I'm not going to get married.' . . . It doesn't fit with human nature. . . . Revolution is not just for single people." Leila expects her marriage, however, to set a "revolutionary example." She will have neither house, children ("in this stage"), nor conventional housewife duties. "We are not ordinary people," she says. But she and her husband, fellow commando Bassem (his last name is kept secret), are "giving society some symbols—actual individuals who are breaking with the harem mentality."

Why are women so effective?

Mona Saudi believes women in the fedayeen movement are more devoted. "Most men are concerned with political revolution. Then by education on the front they realize it should be a social revolution. But women who have been oppressed feel the problems more so they can act and take a position according to their feelings."

Leila Khaled attributes women's effectiveness to the fact that "women are more cold-blooded than men." She continues, "A girl can go secretly for sabotage missions—to hijack or plant mines for example—because . . . women are not as nervous. Of course both men and women get nervous but the women don't show it."

Leila says women make good fighters because they also try harder "to prove they can do the same thing as men and more."[1]

Panache, daring, a reckless lack of concern for innocent lives and refusal to cooperate with the Fatah-dominated fedayeen movement make George Habash's PFLP the enfants terribles of the Arab world. His group is distrusted by the conservative countries—Kuwait, Saudi Arabia, and the oil kingdoms of the Persian Gulf—and Syria whom Habash regards as an enemy. He maintains good relations with Iraq, which is also in conflict with Syria, and has reasonably cordial relations with Egypt which likes to hedge all bets by remaining on good terms with Yasir Arafat's most important competitor.

The PFLP, numbering a few hundred intellectual activists drawn from the largely Christian Palestinian middle class, sees "worldwide imperialism" as the "monster" that together with Zionism is devouring Palestine. The PFLP is committed rhetorically to both overthrowing bourgeois and reactionary regimes and driving the Zionists out of Israel. It regards itself as part of the world revolutionary forces, allied with the struggles of the Vietcong, the Communist Chinese and the national liberation movements of Third World nations in Africa and Asia. The PFLP is against the U.S. as the prime Western "imperialist" and supporter of Israel.

The PFLP was strongly attacked in the Arab world for blowing up the Western-owned petroleum Tapline in the Syrian Golan Heights. Saudi Arabia even threatened to suspend its financial grants to the fedayeen. Fatah opposes taking part in conflicts within the Arab world and does not believe in fighting "reactionary" Arab regimes or American "imperialists" since these diversions weaken the main struggle—liberating Palestine.

The PFLP is challenged on its own ideological grounds by the small and poorly financed Popular Democratic Front for the Liberation of Palestine, which patterns itself on the example of the Maoist Vietcong guerrillas. The main theme of Hawatmeh's political philosophy is that the Mideast conflict is not between Jew and Arab, but is actually a class conflict with the oppressed classes of both sides prevented from recognizing their true interests by the "imperialist" upper classes. Hawatmeh sends missionaries among Arab villagers and Palestinian refugees to explain the class theory. He teaches that not all Jews are bad and that the revolution seeks to replace Israel with a "truly democratic, Socialist state where Jewish and Arab workers will live in harmony." Hawatmeh rejects the notion of a bi-national Palestinian-Jewish state, which is endorsed by some Israeli leftists. The PDFLP says the bourgeois and reactionary Arab armies and governments cannot rectify the Palestinian problem. The only solution, it teaches, is to truly revolutionize Arab society. All Arabs, not only Palestinians, must become freedom fighters on the scale of the Vietcong.

The PDFLP has been embraced by several foreign leftist parties and revolutionary groups who seize upon Hawatmeh's statements to prove that not all fedayeen intend to massacre the Jews living in Israel. The advocates of the PDFLP choose to ignore the threat of politicide implicit in Hawatmeh's message. Once the Jewish state is abolished Hawatmeh's followers are asking the two and a half million Jews in Israel to trust to the good faith of the Arab revolutionaries to guarantee their security and equal rights as a "liberated people." The experience of the Jews in the Middle East, not to mention the Communist revolutions in the Soviet Union and Poland, understandably do not recommend the PDFLP to most Jews, even those desirous of reaching a peaceful and equitable accommodation with the displaced Palestinians.

Ideological inconsistencies, vagueness, and contradictions notwithstanding, the world can expect the Palestinian liberation movement to become more and more entangled in verbal wrangling. Lack of military success against Israel and the debacle in Jordan have forced the movement to turn in on itself. The fedayeen concept of revolutionary warfare has become an increasingly acceptable form of Arab propaganda and strategy because of the radicalization process going on in the Arab world. The emergence of militant Arab revolutionary leaders, such as Colonel Qaddhafi of Libya, striving to fill the void left by Nasser, will encourage the radical fedayeen, and it is unlikely that any moderating influence will prevail in the movement until the Arab world on the whole emerges from what may be a long cycle of political convulsions, revolution and counterrevolution.

NOTES

1. Material on and quotes from Leila Khaled and Mona Saudi taken from: Paula Stern, "A Puzzling New Breed of Arab Woman," *Alicia Patterson Newsletter*, New York, July, 1971.

Fatah leader Yasir Arafat (center) holds news conference in Jordan. On the right is Naif Hawatmeh, chief of the Maoist Popular Democratic Front for the Liberation of Palestine. *(Courtesy of Ha'aretz)*

"Zeev," leading Israeli political cartoonist, comments on fedayeen attacks against El Al planes. Seated at travel agency desk is Yasir Arafat. *(Courtesy of Ha'aretz)*

Former Israeli Chief of Staff, Lt. Gen. Haim Bar-Lev (left) tours Gaza refugee area with Minister of Defense Moshe Dayan. (*Israel Army photo*)

Dr. George Habash, leader of the Popular Front for the Liberation of Palestine.

Fatma Barnavi inspects Israeli magazine account of her attempt to blow up Jerusalem's Zion Cinema.
(*Courtesy Ha'aretz*)

Miriam Sharshir, member of the Popular Democratic Front for the Liberation of Palestine, at Israeli prison.
(*Photo by Zeev Schiff*)

Israeli border patrol searches for fedayeen infiltrators.
(*Photo by Zeev Schiff*)

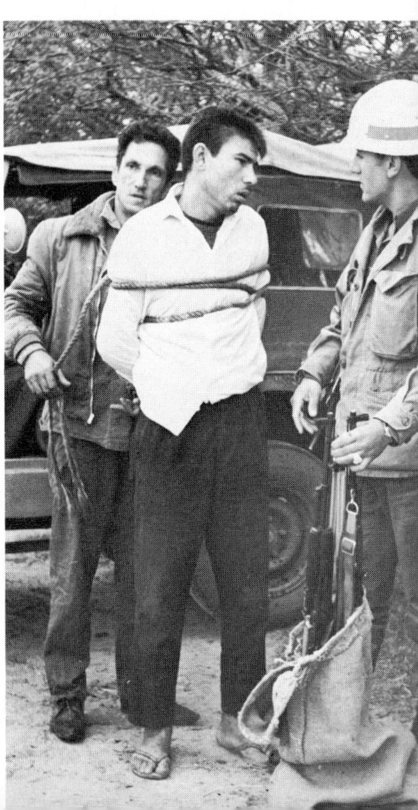

Israeli military police question West-Bank Arab found with Soviet-made automatic rifles.
(*Israel Army photo*)

Suspected fedayeen collaborators in Lebanese village are blindfolded before being taken to Israel command post for interrogation.
(*Photo by Zeev Schiff*)

Elders at Druze village in Southern Lebanon welcome Israeli army unit during reprisal action in Fatahland. (*Photo by Zeev Schiff*)

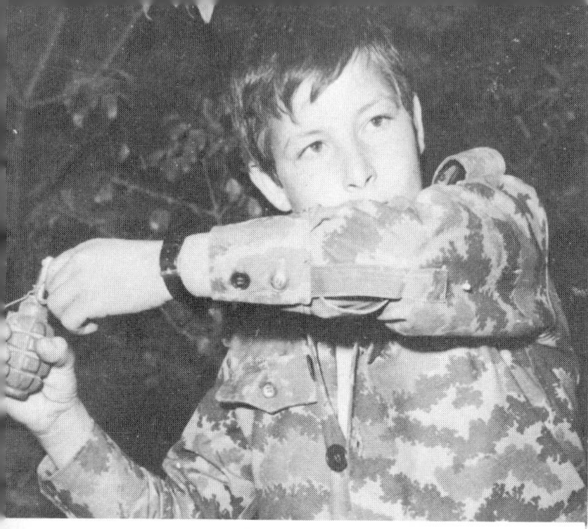

Two fedayeen "Lion Cubs."

Chinese-made stake mine is triggered when stepped on. This was found in Jordan valley.
(*Israel Army photo*)

Fatah squad receives combat instruction in fedayeen camp.
(*Courtesy of Ha'aretz*)

House in northern Israeli village destroyed by Lebanon-based fedayeen rockets. *(Courtesy of Ha'aretz)*

Israeli soldier prepares to blow up collaborator's home in southern Lebanon. *(Photo by Zeev Schiff)*

Israeli soldier searches captured fedayeen. (*Photo by Zeev Schiff*)

Jerusalem supermarket after explosion carried out by fedayeen terrorists. Two persons were killed.
(*Courtesy of Ha'aretz*)

CHAPTER 8

Fedayeen Ideology

The motivation underlying the doctrines of all fedayeen organization stems from the frustration and disappointments the Palestinian Arabs have suffered in their opposition to the Jewish settlement of Palestine, and later, Israel. Their refusal to accept and reach an accommodation with the Jewish State has led them to extremist ideologies that deny the existence of a Jewish national entity as exemplified in Israel.

Israelis are depicted in fedayeen propaganda as members of a religious sect whose followers have been enjoined to settle in Palestine. An attempt is made to create a distinction between Zionists and Jews, as if the former are a separate group of nationalists and the latter a universal people not responsible for the destiny of the State of Israel.

The ultimate aim of the fedayeen is the destruction of the State of Israel and, consequently, they are opposed to any peace agreement between Israel and the Arabs or any compromise settlement. Fedayeen ideology is presented to the Arab people in such terms that the only choice for the Arab nation is to participate in the destruction of Israel or face the degeneration of the Arab peoples. There is no future for the Arabs without Palestine, the fedayeen stress in their publications. The liberation of Palestine is presented as the salvation of the Arabs: all problems will be solved and the Arabs will find unity through the annihilation of the "Zionist State." Facing an inevitable and decisive war with the Jews is considered a primary obligation of Palestinians and all other Arabs.

The Jews of Palestine are described as colonialists, "foreign invaders." There is never any mention in fedayeen writings that there was always a Jewish settlement in Palestine and the many publications of the Palestinian terrorist groups also omit the historical fact that Palestine as a geographical unit was a relatively late development brought into being by the colonial powers at the end of the First World War when the Ottoman Empire was dismembered. Previously, Palestine had been considered part of Syria. Indeed, there was a period when the Arabs of Palestine did not call themselves Palestinians for fear that this would violate the principle of pan-Arabic nationhood. They called themselves "Arabs of southern Syria."

The war with Israel, according to fedayeen ideology, cannot be effectively fought by the existing established Arab armies. Only a revolutionary armed struggle based on guerrilla warfare and enjoying the people's support can bring about the liberation of Palestine. Israel will not be defeated by one sudden military thrust. Rather, the fedayeen argue, the revolution will have the effect of both providing the catalyst for the transformation of Arab society and the destruction of the various military, political, economic and intellectual institutions of the "Zionist occupation state."

"The Jewish State," one fedayeen source declares, "is an aberrant, mistaken phenomenon in our nation's history and therefore there is no alternative but to wipe out the existential trace of this artificial phenomenon."

The fedayeen have sought to avoid the use of extremist rhetoric that promises genocide. Such expressions as "throwing the Jews into the sea," which were popular with Ahmed Shukairy and Arab leaders before the Six-Day War, produced world-wide moral revulsion. The fedayeen have been more subtle: they speak of wiping out the Zionist State but also of allowing the Jews to remain as a minority in a democratic Arab Palestine. What is never satisfactorily explained by the fedayeen ideologists is how the Zionist entity can be destroyed without massacring or driving out the people belonging to that entity. In his profound study of fedayeen strategy,[1] Y. Harkabi writes that when the implications of the fedayeen objective are spelled out "it is realized that Zionism is not only a political regime or a superstructure of sorts, but is embodied in a *society* [Harkabi's emphasis]. Therefore, this society has to be liquidated, which underlines that achieving it will require a great deal of killing. The Arabs' objective of destroying the State of Israel (what may be called a 'politicide') drives them to genocide."

In essence, then, the fedayeen are continuing the

Arab strategy of seeking the abolition of Israel and the elimination of the Jewish presence from the Middle East. By adopting the tactic of guerrilla war the Palestinian militants say they will be able to achieve the destruction of the Zionist State but they are vague on details of how their guerrilla struggle can defeat a determined country like Israel whose successful army represents the people's will to survive as citizens of a Jewish nation.

Fedayeen attach considerable significance to their guerrilla struggle. It is regarded as the vehicle for a total Arab revolution and the subsequent democratizing and socialization of Arab life. In contrast to Mao Tse-tung and other theorists who saw the guerrilla war as a tactical stage leading to a decisive all-out struggle, the fedayeen view the guerrilla war as an ultimate and overall strategy. There are many inconsistencies in the writings and pronouncements of the fedayeen as to whether the Palestinians are capable of achieving the liberation of Palestine by themselves. While armed struggle is cited as the factor that will galvanize the Palestinian masses, who are "irresistible," and can free the "usurped" homeland, there is also recognition that the final blow will have to be struck by the joint Arab forces.

Fedayeen ideology dictates that the war with Israel is total—against her army and civilians and in hostile opposition to the entire fabric of Israeli society. Thus, terrorism is the instrument of warfare against civilian institutions. Every Israeli—and frequently Jews abroad—are considered proper targets.

Violence is exalted in fedayeen literature and announcements as the means of wiping out the Jewish "colonialist" presence and as a unifying force for the Arab people. The thinking of Frantz Fanon, the Algerian theorist of revolution and violence whose book *The Wretched of the Earth* has attracted international attention, has had considerable impact on the Palestinian extremists. Fanon's concept of the psychological value of violence to oppressed people is enthusiastically embraced by the fedayeen who see in terrorism and killing a release from their frustrations and a path of redemption for the inferiority complex engendered by their degraded circumstances. Shortly before the Six-Day War, Fatah sent a memo to journalists stating, "Blazing our armed revolution inside the occupied territory (i.e., Israel) is a healing medicine for all our people's diseases." In one of Fatah's pamphlets titled "The Revolution and Violence—The Road to Victory," the following statement is made: "This is a war of annihilation of one of the rivals, either wiping out the national entity [Palestine], or wiping out colonialism . . . The enslaved will be liberated from violence by violence."

The rejection of any peaceful solution of the Mideast conflict or of the possibility of co-existence with Israel is a central fedayeen doctrine and it is a mistake to think that the leftist Palestinian guerrilla groups are more liberal and understanding. The most leftist fedayeen groups give their unyielding position an ideological justification in Marxist terms in addition to the nationalistic message. At a March, 1970, symposium of fedayeen organizations, later reported in the Lebanese newspaper *Al Anwar*, the delegate of the Popular Democratic Front for the Liberation of Palestine (the group thought to be the most leftist) said: "Co-existence with the Israeli entity is impossible, not only because of Arab nationalistic aspirations, but because the existence of such an entity would dictate this area's pattern of development based on the link between international imperialism and Zionism. Therefore, uprooting the imperialist influence in the Middle East means uprooting the Israeli entity. This aim cannot be relinquished—not only because of the Palestinian right of self-determination in its homeland, but because of considerations of the overall Arab liberation movement."

The official Palestinian liberation movement doctrine is expressed in the Palestinian National Covenant consisting of thirty-three articles. It was originally drawn up at the first Palestinian Congress, which took place in the former Jordanian sector of Jerusalem on May 19, 1964. The Covenant was revised to reflect Fatah's thinking on the post Six-Day War situation and made more extreme in several respects by the Palestinian National Council, which met in Cairo in July, 1968, with the participation of fedayeen representatives.

The main principles of the revised charter of Covenant concerning the Jews and Israel state that in the future Palestinian state only Jews who lived in Palestine before 1917 (the year of the Balfour declaration and, according to the Arabs, the beginning of the "Zionist invasion") will be recognized as citizens (Article 6). In the earlier version it was stated: "Jews of Palestinian origin will be considered Palestinians if they are willing to endeavor to live in loyalty and peace in Palestine." Although the phrasing of the 1964 version is vague since there is no definition of what a Jew of "Palestinian origin" is, the more recent version makes it quite clear that the return of the Palestinian Arabs means the removal of Jews already living in Israel since most of them came there after 1917.

Articles 3 and 21 of the 1968 Covenant stress that only the Palestinian Arabs possess the right of self-determination, and the entire country belongs to them. Article 3 states: "The Palestinian Arab people possesses the legal right to its homeland, and when the liberation of its homeland is completed it will exercise self-determination solely according to its own will and choice."

Article 21 states: "The Palestinian Arab people, in expressing itself through the armed Palestinian revolution, rejects every solution that is a substitute for a complete liberation of Palestine, and rejects plans that aim at the settlement of the Palestine issue or its internationalization."

The Covenant also rejects the internationally sanctioned partition of the disputed area and refuses to recognize the legality of the United Nations decision of November, 1947, partitioning Palestine into Jewish and Arab states (the latter decision was rejected by the Palestinian Arabs under the influence of the Arab nations who invaded Palestine to prevent Israel from coming into being).

Article 20 says: "The Balfour Declaration, the Mandate document and what has been based upon them are considered null and void. The claim of a historical or spiritual tie between Jews and Palestine does not tally with historical realities nor with the constituents of statehood in their own true sense. Judaism, in its character as a religion of revelation, is not a nationality with an independent existence. Likewise, the Jews are not one people with an independent personality. They are rather citizens of the state to which they belong."

Thus, while claiming the right of self-determination for themselves, the Palestinians presume to tell the Jews what they are and are not.

Article 9 unequivocally expresses the fedayeen commitment to violence: "Armed struggle is the only way to liberate Palestine and is therefore a strategy and not tactics. The Palestinian Arab people affirms its absolute resolution and abiding determination to pursue the armed struggle and to march forward toward the armed popular revolution, to liberate its homeland and return to it, [to maintain] its right to a natural life in it, and to exercise its right of self-determination in it and sovereignty over it."

Article 15 states the two-fold goal of the "armed Palestinian revolution"—defending the rest of the Arab world and removing Zionism from Palestine. "The liberation of Palestine, from an Arab viewpoint, is a national duty to repulse the Zionist, imperialist invasion from the great Arab homeland and to purge the Zionist presence from Palestine. Its full responsibilities fall upon the Arab nation, peoples and governments, with the Palestinian Arab people at their head."[2]

The determination to wipe out the physical entity of the Jewish state and any trace of its civilization is common to all fedayeen doctrines. But the apparent contradiction of ridding Palestine of two and a half million Jews, as implied in the Covenant and the declaration that the aim of the Palestinian revolution is to replace the Zionist state with a multinational, democratic Palestinian state in which Moslems, Christians, and Jews would live together has not been dealt with by any Arab group even though it arouses considerable skepticism abroad as to the fedayeen's true aims regarding the Jews. An indication of actual fedayeen thinking on the question of the Jews in Israel is provided by Shafik El-Hut, one of the leaders of the Palestine Liberation Organization. He says: "Regarding the humanitarian position concerning the Jews, this must be expressed in such a way that we expose the Zionist movement and say to the Jews that the Zionist movement that brought them to Israel did not solve their problems as Jews and they must return to their place of origin in order to find another way to solve the problem of Jewish persecution in the world. The Jew has no choice but to assimilate in his society."[3]

The idealized cultural and religious pluralism the fedayeen boast of does not apparently apply to the Jews who are asked to give up their national identity.

In a Fatah pamphlet of October, 1968, which was distributed in English at the University of California, Berkeley in 1969, the following is found: "Fatah is the armed humanitarian movement whose goal is the freeing of the Jews from their nationalistic and Nazi enslavement and the finding of a *final solution* [emphasis ours] for the Jewish problem." The Fatah bulletin goes on to suggest that if the Jews of Middle Eastern origin were to return to their countries of origin—something Fatah claims they want to do—the problem would, in large measure, be solved. The article then calls on the nations of the world to cooperate in absorbing the Jews who are living "illegally" in Palestine. Fatah's use of the term "final solution" can only have unpleasant associations for Jews old enough to remember Auschwitz and Dachau. It reveals, however, the true intentions of the fedayeen far more than any of their propaganda about pluralistic, secular states.

Fatah has shown itself to be less than comfortable with emphasis on the secular part of the slogan "a democratic and secular Palestine." This slogan was mainly the creation of the New Left rather than Fatah. The latter found it convenient to keep the myth alive because of the response it elicits in radical circles abroad who prefer to think the Palestinian "war of liberation" is striving for a humane resolution of the Palestine problem and seeks a non-theocratic state to replace Israel, which radical and fedayeen propaganda depicts as an "exclusivist, anachronistic" state founded upon a "religious principle."

Anna Frankus, a French-Jewish writer who has done much to popularize the fedayeen in European leftist publications, including *Jeune Afrique*, trumpeted the idea of the secular state apparently because she felt that just declaring the need to destroy the Jewish character of Israel would not be considered a progressive aim among members of the extreme European and American Left. For the benefit of Arab audiences, Yasir Arafat disavowed the secularist aim in an interview in an Egyptian newspaper in June, 1970, when he said: "We formulated the slogan calling for the creation of a democratic state in Palestine in which Moslems, Christians, and Jews would live. But we are not responsible for the motto calling for the establishment of a secular state. What happened is that the French writer, Anna Frankus, author of the book *The Palestinians*, spread this slogan in the name of the Palestinian revolution in several of her articles. I am certain, however, that this is a distortion of the expression of democracy we proclaim."

Fedayeen confusion on the vision of a democratic Palestinian state is indicated by Fatah's refusal to give details on how the projected state would work and the expressions of disappointment by the more leftist fedayeen groups who see a lack of firm support for the democratic ideal. In a publication of the Popular Democratic Front for the Liberation of Palestine (September, 1969) the following commentary appeared: "Even generalized slogans as 'a democratic state,' have been rejected by the Palestinian National Council. Clear racist tendencies have been detected in the ranks of the Right regarding the question of Israel and the reactionary solutions offered are close in nature to those of Ahmed Shukairy [the deposed leader of the Palestine Liberation Organization]."

The PDFLP concept of a democratic Palestine can be derived from a proposal it made at the Sixth Palestine National Council meeting: "The national liberation movement will achieve a popular, democratic Palestinian state only through armed struggle and popular liberation war against Zionism and reactionary imperialism and the destruction of the Jewish state and the liberation of the Jews from the Zionist movement. Because of ties of history and destiny between Palestine and the Arab nation the popular democratic Palestinian state will be an organic part of the Arab federation of the Middle East; a democratic state hostile to colonialism, imperialism, Zionism, and to Arab and Palestinian forces of reaction."

The refusal of the Palestine liberation movement to recognize Jewish national claims and rights as expressed in the Zionist movement precludes the possibility of any realistic settlement of the Palestinian plight. Calling for a return to their homeland by annihilating or dispersing a Jewish population with deep spiritual and cultural ties to that land is, at best, wishful thinking; at worst, suicidal.

NOTES

1. Y. Harkabi, *Fedayeen Action and Arab Strategy*, The Institute For Strategic Studies, London, 1968.
2. Translation of the 1968 Palestinian National Covenant articles from the Arabic by J. Kraemer as it appears in Y. Harkabi's paper, "The Position of the Palestinians in the Israel-Arab Conflict and Their National Covenant (1968)," Tel Aviv, 1969.
3. Reported in *Al Anwar*, Beirut, March, 1970.

CHAPTER 9

Terrorism Abroad

*On July 18, 1968, a man dressed as a priest en*tered the Rome office of El Al Israel Airlines. He presented three passports—one Indian and two issued by Iran—and purchased three tickets from Rome to Tel Aviv. A few days later, shortly after 1:00 A.M. on the night of July 23, an El Al Boeing 707 took off from Rome airport headed for Lydda airport near Tel Aviv. Aboard were thirty-eight passengers and ten crew members. Twenty of the passengers were not Israelis and included a group of seven Catholic priests on a pilgrimage to the Holy Land. Also among the non-Israeli passengers were three travelers whose tickets had been bought five days earlier by the man pretending to be a priest. These three opened a new chapter in the fedayeen war of terrorism against Israel.

El Al Flight #426—Paris-Tel Aviv via Rome—never arrived at its destination. In what was the first of several international hijackings carried out against Israeli and non-Israeli airlines by Palestinian guerrillas, Flight #426 was diverted to Algeria. The Palestinian war against Israel was no longer confined to the borders of the Middle East. A new front extending well beyond the Mediterranean had opened.

Twenty minutes after takeoff from Rome, passengers heard gun fire coming from the cockpit. A few minutes later one of the Israeli pilots came stumbling into the passenger section, his face covered with blood. He had tried to disarm the hijackers and in the struggle was struck on the head and face by a revolver butt. The hijackers had sat quietly in the first-class cabin until by prearranged signal they jumped up and forced their way into the pilots' section. After ordering the crew to head for Algeria, two of the terrorists came out to confront the passengers who were astounded by the men, one brandishing a revolver and the other carrying a hand grenade. The latter warned in halting English: "If you don't sit still, we'll all go . . ." And with a cynical smile his comrade added: "We are your cousins. We are men of Palestine."

The passengers were ordered to place their hands on their heads and the hijackers kept up a nervous flow of chatter. One proposed to the Catholic pilgrims that they pray. "Perhaps God will heed your prayer," he said and then stepped over to the wounded pilot. In a grotesque gesture he rubbed his finger in the blood congealing around the Israeli's cuts and bruises. Then sucking his blood-stained finger he said, "How tasty and good is the blood of Jews."

The Captain was watched by a hijacker who displayed professional familiarity with the plane's instruments and radio. After a smooth landing at Maison Blanche airport in Algeria, the Israelis were separated from the others and taken to an army camp near the airport. The non-Israelis were freed and allowed to leave by other flights.

Although the Algerians may not have wanted to get involved in the illegal act of pirating a civil aircraft, they cooperated with the fedayeen once the plane was on their territory. The organ of the revolutionary Algerian regime, *Al Mujahid*, praised the seizure of the El Al plane and claimed that the Israeli airline is not like other civil aviation companies but a "military instrument" and therefore a legitimate target for Palestinian commandos. Other Arab regimes also spoke out in support of the hijacking. A Lebanese newspaper commented: "The hijacking of an El Al plane is piracy, but this is legal and revolutionary piracy."

In Israel the public was outraged but the government was impotent in the face of the daring fedayeen action. Israel could choose between acquiescing in this Palestinian power play or take drastic reprisals against Arab civil aviation, a step she was reluctant to take even though it could be accomplished fairly easily. Worldwide reaction to this crime against international aviation was surprisingly apathetic and once the non-Israeli passengers were released, pressure on the Algerian government abated. The United Nations contented itself with an insipid declaration deploring the incident and talk of actual protests by the International Air Transport Association and International Pilots Association came to nothing. Government statements deploring the incident were all careful not to lay blame on the Algerians.

In the absence of firm and determined action, the Palestinians and other political extremists were encouraged to continue hijacking as a means of warfare. This tactic was to reach a high point in September, 1970, when three jet liners of different nations were hijacked to Jordan and 310 passengers were held hostage in the desert by members of the Popular Front for the Liberation of Palestine. The three planes were destroyed in Jordan and a fourth, a Pan American jumbo jet, was subsequently blown up at Cairo airport.

The hijacking to Algeria of the El Al Boeing was a psychological and propaganda victory for the fedayeen in the eyes of the Arabs. The disapproval of international public opinion had no effect on the terrorists who were determined to dramatize their cause. Their failure to score any impressive military achievements against Israel in the months after the Six-Day War had led some observers in Israel to expect a highly visible and daring escapade. It was natural that following their failure to establish bases and underground cells in the occupied territories, some fedayeen groups would seek other avenues of activity where they could avoid Israel's defense forces and the restraints of host Arab governments.

Another reason for the extension of the struggle against Israel beyond the geographic limits of the Mideast was the competition between fedayeen organizations. Yasir Arafat's Fatah was receiving most of the attention of the world press. In order to justify their existence, other groups also had to gain publicity for their real and imagined exploits. Unable to achieve this by guerrilla action directly aimed at Israel, some groups chose extreme and sensational methods. Merely laying a strip of mines along an Israeli border road was not sufficient. An action that strikes at vulnerable civilian air traffic is tailor-made for the purposes of a small band of reckless militants anxious for publicity.

Dr. George Habash's Popular Front for the Liberation of Palestine was unable to compete with Fatah in conventional guerrilla and terrorist harassment and chose attacks on civilian air installations as an alternative. At first, action was confined to Israeli planes and terminals, but later was broadened to include American jets and those of other countries. The justification, according to Habash, was that the United States was an ally of Israel and the other nations also maintained relations with the "Zionist State."

Habash and his followers hoped that by acts of extreme violence involving innocent persons the plight of the Palestinians would be revived as a major international concern. Habash has said the murder of one Jew where it will provoke shock and outrage is better than killing ten Israeli soldiers in a border incident. In September, 1969, a spokesman for the PFLP said at a news conference in Amman, Jordan: "The Popular Front plans an all-out war against Zionism outside of the Middle East, without regard for the lives of citizens in foreign countries. The Front will not be responsible for the lives of tourists and foreign travelers using Israeli travel facilities.

The Front had earlier shown its disregard for civilian lives, including women and children, by planting explosives in buses, cinemas, and supermarkets. At one stage a public debate over the morality of attacking civilians was carried on in the Arab press. Habash and his supporters, including many members of Al Fatah, resolved the debate in their minds with the following reasoning: "We are not attacking innocent civilians, only military personnel. One must take into consideration the fact that practically every Israeli male serves in the reserves and must be regarded as a soldier." The presence of women and children aboard El Al flights in addition to non-Jews and citizens of nations not involved in the Mideast dispute was not dealt with by the PFLP.

Habash and the leaders of the extremist Marxist-Leninist groups that had broken away from his tutelage scorned Yasir Arafat's disapproval of terrorist acts against civilian targets outside of the borders of Israel by insisting that Israel's interests must be attacked everywhere.

This policy was behind the PFLP attack on the Western-owned petroleum Tapline in the occupied Golan Heights and the hijackings of American and European jets.

The El Al plane and passengers who were hijacked to Algeria were held for a month. During that time pressure on Algeria grew increasingly weak and Israel felt isolated in her attempt to save her civilians and aircraft. The experience strengthened Jerusalem's conviction that she would have to take far-reaching measures in her own behalf or face a constant threat to her civil aviation. Thanks to Italy acting as an intermediary, the Algerian regime finally consented to release the plane and passengers in return for the freeing of several fedayeen held in Israeli jails.

The PFLP regarded the hijacking as a great success and saw that no matter how outraged world reactions to the hijacking were, they did not go beyond words. There was no move to boycott the airports of the Arab nations harboring Palestinian revolutionary groups. The PFLP was thus encouraged to pursue its policy of terrorizing international air travel facilities.

On December 26, 1968, an El Al plane parked on the runway at Athens International Airport was attacked by two Palestinian youths from Lebanon. Armed with a machine gun and hand grenades, the two terrorists approached the plane as it was about to take off with both Israeli and non-Israeli passengers and opened fire at close-range at the cockpit and passenger sections. Leon Shirdan, an Israeli engineer employed by the United Nations, was killed in the attack. The fedayeen were seized and arrested by the Greek authorities.

This time Israel reacted drastically. She knew that the verbal protests of the International Pilots Association had little meaning because the pilots were under the impression that only Israeli planes were vulnerable to terrorist attacks. The Israeli government was aware that the Arab nations supporting the fedayeen were in favor of the hijackings and other forms of terrorism while at the same time declaring themselves free of responsibility for the outrages. Israel refused to concede the right of the Arab governments to actively support fedayeen without being held accountable for the deeds of their protégés. In the case of the hijacking to Algeria and the Athens incident, Lebanon was the country of origin of the fedayeen who carried out the attacks and in Israel's eyes Beirut bore a heavy responsibility for harboring Palestinian extremists.

But no less guilty were Egypt and Syria who aided the Palestinian guerrillas and were pressuring the Greek government to cancel the legal proceedings against the two Arabs who had attacked the El Al jet and killed an Israeli civilian. Cairo and Damascus sent lawyers to defend the accused fedayeen and the ambassadors of both countries were present at the trials which resulted in light prison sentences. The Greeks were subject to Egyptian pressure because of extensive Greek interests in the Middle East and the pro-Arab views of its foreign ministry at the time.

On December 28, Israel retaliated at night with a strike at Beirut airport carried out by a helicopter-borne raiding party. The action began with Israeli commandos gathering all travelers and airport personnel in the airport's main hall where they were guarded until the counter-sabotage was completed. The planes of Arab air lines were the target and the purpose of the raid was to demonstrate to the Arabs that their civil carriers were no less vulnerable than Israel's and that fedayeen provocations would be answered two-fold. While 1500 onlookers crowded terraces and observation decks for a view, the Israeli soldiers blew up fourteen planes belonging to Lebanon's Mideast Airways and other Arab lines. The damage was estimated afterward at $100 million. Lebanese troops did not attack the Israeli unit and the withdrawal was completed with no injuries.

This time the United Nations acted with an alacrity that had not been evident when Israeli planes and lives were involved. Within three days of the Beirut Airport reprisal the Security Council, which is dominated by pro-Soviet and pro-Arab nations that do not have diplomatic relations with Israel, passed a resolution condemning the Israeli action. This was followed by France announcing that she was extending her anti-Israel embargo to include not only jets already bought and paid for but other military equipment and spare parts. The French press reported that President de Gaulle was angry over the fact that the Israeli action had been carried out with French-made helicopters. The U.N. resolution and French displeasure over the blow aimed at Lebanon, a highly Gallicized former French protectorate with special protégé status in de Gaulle's eyes, was construed in Israel as meaning that the fedayeen would be further encouraged in their terrorism. No such stern and forceful protests had followed the killing of an innocent Israeli in Athens or the hijacking of the El Al Boeing to Algeria.

On February 18, 1969, the next Palestinian assault

took place at Zurich airport. Four saboteurs, including a girl, waited for an El Al plane to ready itself for takeoff before opening fire with automatic weapons and tossing hand grenades. This time El Al security was on the alert. Mordechai Rahamim, a plainclothes guard, leaped from the plane and shot and killed the leader of the band, Muhasan Abdul, thirty-one, bearer of a Jordanian passport. The three other fedayeen were arrested by Swiss police as was Rahamim. Two of the crew members were injured and one of them, a trainee pilot, later died from his wounds. The aim of the terrorists was clearly to kill as many crew and passengers—Israelis and other nationals—as possible. They had fired at the plane's full fuel tanks with incendiary bullets and the grenades they threw were also of the incendiary type. These facts contradict fedayeen claims that their intention was to destroy the plane only after the passengers had been removed. A leaflet found in the automobile used by the terrorists declared: "We have acted in the spirit of Wilhelm Tell who stood at the head of the Swiss national resistance. Due to extreme circumstances beyond our control we were forced to violate Switzerland's neutrality."

The Palestinians were tried and sentenced to long prison terms. Rahamim was exonerated.

The incident revealed for the first time that Israel was protecting El Al crews and passengers by training and stationing civilian security men on every flight and at every terminal. The appearance of Israeli security personnel gave rise to second thoughts on the part of the PFLP activists and from that time forward efforts were made to avoid confrontations with plainclothes Israeli guards. A new strategy calling for attacking passengers before they boarded their planes was introduced and non-Israeli carriers were selected as targets because of the absence of special security men aboard their flights. Eventually El Al's planes became the safest traveling international air routes. Other countries began to pay the price for their failure to act firmly to adopt measures against the Palestinian air terrorists and the Arab states sponsoring them.

The American carrier, Trans World Airlines, was the first non-Israeli company to be struck by George Habash's militants. On August 29, 1969, Leila Khaled and two male companions boarded the TWA Los Angeles-Tel Aviv flight during its stopover in Athens and hijacked the Boeing 707 to Damascus where its cockpit was blown up. Leila recalled in an interview afterwards that the hijacking had been easy and there is no reason to doubt her word since once hijackers manage to board a plane with weapons their chances of success are excellent. Pilots will not risk the lives of their passengers by refusing to obey an armed person holding a pistol or larger firearm. Six Israelis were aboard the TWA flight—four women and two adult males. The women were released but the men, both civilians—one a professor of medicine at the Hebrew University and the other a businessman—were held for several months illegally by the Syrians in a military prison. They were finally exchanged for several Syrian soldiers who had been taken prisoner on Israeli territory.

The success of the TWA hijacking encouraged other fedayeen groups to follow the lead of the PFLP.

On February 2, 1970, one of the groups that had broken away from the PFLP, Ahmed Jibril's Popular Front for the Liberation of Palestine—General Command, planted a bomb aboard a Swissair plane bound for Tel Aviv. The jet exploded in midair over Switzerland, killing all forty-seven passengers and crew members. Among the victims were sixteen Israelis, including a noted heart surgeon who had frequently treated Arab patients from Israel, the occupied territories and Arab countries.

On the same day, an explosive device planted in a bag of Israel-bound mail aboard an Austrian plane enroute from Frankfurt, West Germany to Vienna went off and tore a hole in a section of the aircraft. The pilot was, however, able to land safely. A subsequent investigation revealed that two Arabs in Frankfurt had mailed a package containing explosives concealed inside a portable transistor radio and a pressure gauge that acted as a detonator when the air pressure in the cabin reached a certain point.

On the evening of February 2, Abu Maryim, one of the commanders of the PFLP—GC broadcast a communique from Beirut admitting responsibility for the explosion of the Swissair jet. That night the BBC reported from Amman that the Swissair tragedy had occurred because the PFLP—GC had decided to strike out everywhere. Ahmed Jibril, however, assumed a more cautious tone and asserted that Israeli "experts" had been aboard the plane. In Switzerland it was disclosed that a week before the explosion, the Swiss Embassy in Beirut had received a letter threatening to kidnap Swiss ambassadors unless a new trial was held for the fedayeen convicted of attacking the El Al plane in Zurich a year earlier.

A few months prior to the Swissair attack, three fedayeen from Syria fired at passengers at Munich airport who were preparing to board an El Al plane at the conclusion of a short stopover. One of Israel's leading actresses, Hannah Meron, was badly wounded and had to have a leg amputated. Among the passengers was the actor son of Moshe Dayan, Assaf, who was enroute to England to make a film.

In Athens in November, 1969, fedayeen belonging to a small Jordan-based group called the Popular Struggle Front threw grenades at the El Al office. Fourteen persons, mostly Greeks, were injured and a Greek infant was killed. One of the two terrorists was a Jordanian studying medicine in Greece. Despite public anger over the crime, the Greek government released the two Palestinians from Lebanon who had killed the Israeli engineer aboard an El Al plane in December, 1968, and the two youths from Jordan responsible for the murder of the Greek child in response to the demands of fedayeen who hijacked an Olympic Airlines jet in July, 1970. By giving in to blackmail Greece set a dangerous precedent, one that was to spur further acts of hijackings to secure the release of jailed Arab terrorists.

Just two months later, on September 6, 1970, members of the Popular Front for the Liberation of Palestine hijacked four planes belonging to Swissair, Pan American, TWA, and BOAC. An attempted hijacking of an El Al plane was unsuccessful and resulted in the death of Patrick Joseph Arguello, an American radical who was Leila Khaled's comrade.

In this mass offensive, the most spectacular escapade in the history of aerial hijacking, 310 civilian hostages—Jews, Israelis, Americans, British, Dutch, Germans, and others—were brought to a remote strip of Jordanian Desert known as "Dawson's Field" to wait anxiously for international bargaining to free them. The hijackings of September were a precipitating factor in the Jordanian civil war between army and fedayeen which erupted while most of the hostages were still in fedayeen hands. It was a miracle that all the hostages escaped alive from the devastation that hit Amman during the fighting.

The PFLP had demanded the release of Leila

Khaled, who was being held by police in London, three fedayeen who had been arrested in West Germany for the attack on the Munich El Al terminal, and three fedayeen imprisoned in Switzerland for the February, 1969, Zurich airport assault on an El Al liner. An additional demand was the release of an unspecified number of fedayeen in Israeli prisons.

In the aftermath of those confusing and violence-filled days it became clear that Israel had refused to yield to fedayeen blackmail but that Britain, West Germany, and Switzerland had all agreed to the Palestinians' demands and freed the convicted terrorists.[1]

Leila Khaled was taken aboard a Royal Air Force Comet jet on the night of September 30. The next destination was Munich where a trio of her comrades was picked up. At Zurich the remaining three were collected. By morning they were in Cairo in time to attend Nasser's funeral. The Egyptian leader had suffered a fatal heart attack while trying to mediate between Hussein and the fedayeen.

The hijackings had the opposite of the desired propaganda effect. Instead of eliciting sympathy for the fedayeen's cause, their aerial piracy and destruction of jet planes provoked a negative reaction in a world weary of violence and anarchy. Even the fact that the hostages had not been harmed and, by all accounts, had been treated in humane fashion, even during the height of fighting in Jordan, was obscured by the outrage and annoyance felt by people uninvolved in the Arab-Israeli conflict. Men and women favorably disposed to the Palestinians' claims were shocked and repelled by the extremists' capacity to cause ruinous damage.

A few days after Nasser's funeral, Leila Khaled, dressed in a black pants suit and wearing sunglasses, was spotted laying a wreath at the Egyptian president's tomb. A British TV journalist asked her if she felt in "any way responsible for the train of events that led to a Mideast crisis." Leila replied: "Not at all."

"You feel no responsibility, none at all?" the journalist persisted.

"No!" Miss Khaled said and shook her head.[2]

Plane hijacking and attacks on air terminals were only one aspect of the PFLP's campaign of terrorism for export. In Buenos Aires, the Israeli exhibit at a trade show was put on fire and at an international fair in Izmir, Turkey, a Jordanian student was injured when he and an accomplice attempted to set an explosive charge at the Israeli pavilion. In London, a bomb was planted underneath the carpet in the reception area of the Israeli shipping lines offices. There were also a spate of incidents involving Israeli embassies. In Asuncion, capital of Paraguay, two fedayeen broke into the Israeli Embassy and killed an Israeli clerk, the mother of two children, and seriously wounded a local employe. The embassies in Bonn and The Hague were also bombed. The Palestinian groups used junior members for some attacks. Teen-age youths were trained in sabotage techniques and dispatched abroad where they were given instructions by adult fedayeen reluctant to risk their own lives.

In Brussels, two 13-year-old boys were arrested after throwing grenades at an El Al office and injuring four Belgians. In The Hague, investigators of the Israeli Embassy bombing apprehended a 15-year-old responsible for the deed. Leaders of the PFLP told journalists they hoped the youthful terrorists would be put on trial so they could tell the world about the plight of the Palestinian people. They justified sending minors on dangerous missions by asserting that this proved to the world that the new generation of Palestinians had not forgotten their homeland. The boy taken into custody in The Hague, Tiasar Ali Abu Atar, was brought from Amman to West Germany by a 62-year-old Arab and was then taken directly to the entrance of the Israeli Embassy in the Netherlands.

Fedayeen anger was also directed at Jewish communal and private institutions in various parts of the world. In Buenos Aires, home of a large Arab population and the center of anti-Semitic activity in Latin America, a Jewish school was burned. In Prague a synagogue was set afire and in West Germany several elderly Jews, survivors of the Nazi holocaust, were killed when fedayeen fired their old age home. In Paris, the Rothschild bank was attacked and in London fedayeen assaults on Jewish institutions elicited a strong response from a group of pro-Israeli Jewish militants. The Arab terrorists met a similar reaction in New York where the Jewish Defense League threatened to retaliate against Arab diplomats for any acts of Arab terrorism directed at local Jewish and Israeli offices. The spokesman for the P.L.O. in New York, Saadat Hassan, and an aide were severely beaten by what many observers believe was a gang of Jewish Defense League (JDL) zealots. Police and private guards were posted at Israeli government offices and special security measures were taken by pro-Israeli organizations.

The PFLP did not rely solely on its own members for operations abroad. A recruitment program was initiated for mercenaries and radicals knowledgeable in the art of sabotage. Fatah also began looking for experts in various specialities to train its members. A few dozen foreign volunteers joined Fatah and some were killed in training accidents. The identity of one, a French citizen, was given as Roger Cordov who, it was said, was killed in action against Israel. He actually died from a stray bullet during a training exercise.

International adventurers, convicted criminals, and anti-Israel leftist extremists applied to Fatah and PFLP fund-raising and propaganda offices in Europe. In several instances, when PFLP members lacked the necessary skills for certain operations, mercenaries were sent. Perhaps the most publicized non-Arab taking part in Palestinian actions was Patrick Arguello, a native of San Francisco born to an Anglo-Irish mother and a Nicaraguan father who was wanted by several Central American security agencies for subversive activities. Arguello was killed by an Israeli security man while attempting to hijack an El Al plane with Leila Khaled in September, 1970.

Fatah's and the PFLP's camps in Amman became refuge for several wanted criminals who were given asylum once they declared their oppositon to Israel and support of the fedayeen cause.

The PFLP recruited Bruno Bargit, twenty-five, a Swiss citizen who was arrested in Haifa in June, 1970 while carrying concealed explosives and other sabotage equipment. Bargit was invited to join the ranks of the PFLP during a visit to Lebanon. After training in the use of explosives he was promised $6000 for carrying out an operation in Israel involving the planting of explosives in two heavily populated civilian centers. To Israel's security agencies Bargit's mission was nothing new; they had just finished dealing with a group of English criminals who had been recruited to hijack an El Al plane and kidnap several well-known London Jews.

In 1969, the PFLP hired Rolf Swenson, a Swede, to kill former Israeli Premier David Ben-Gurion in South Africa during the latter's stopover there as part of an international lecture tour. Swenson first made contact with

Egyptian intelligence while serving as a member of the United Nations Truce Supervision Organization forces in the Gaza Strip. Following his discharge he is believed to have carried out several espionage missions for the Egyptians. After the Six-Day War, members of the PFLP contacted Swenson and invited him to Beirut, where he entered into an agreement with Habash's group.

He had two partners in the conspiracy to murder Ben-Gurion. One was Mona Saudi who later acted as the fedayeen "hostess" during the September, 1970 hijacking of a BOAC VC-10. Miss Saudi was exhibiting her drawings of Palestinian children in Sweden and Denmark at the time of the Ben-Gurion plot and was known to be friendly with several members of the Swedish New Left. The second partner was Suhil Abdul Razak, a Palestinian with an Iraqi passport.

The original plan was for the trio to fly to South Africa where Swenson, posing as a journalist, would shoot the former Israeli Prime Minister during an airport news conference. The plan was changed because Ben-Gurion left South Africa sooner than expected. A revised strategy called for the assassination to take place at the inevitable airport news conferences in Brazil or Buenos Aires. Mona Saudi was assigned the task of smuggling the weapon to the scene of the murder and Razak was sent along as a watchman. Israeli agents in Scandinavia uncovered the plot two days before it was to be carried out. The Danish police were alerted and the three would-be killers were arrested and subsequently expelled from Denmark.

Several fedayeen attempts to recruit terrorists among sympathetic foreigners have ended quite unhappily for the accomplices. In the summer of 1971 a case was reported in Israel involving girls whose Palestinian friends had persuaded them to commit sabotage in Israel for the fedayeen.

Nadia Bardali, twenty-six, and her younger sister Marilyn, twenty-one, are the daughters of Bashir Bardali, a prosperous Moroccan bus company operator, and a French mother. The girls, both pretty and outgoing, grew up among Casablanca's social elite and until the Six-Day War were friendly with several young Moroccan Jews. Nadia was drawn to the ideas of Europe's New Left and at one time tried to get backing for a Leftist French-language magazine to be called "The Third World."

In 1970, both girls traveled to London where they studied and became friendly with members of the Popular Front for the Liberation of Palestine. They agreed to carry out a mission against Israel and together with a 21-year-old German girl, Evelyn Barage, were caught attempting to smuggle sabotage materials into Israel by hiding explosives in their bras. Evelyn Barage was wanted in Holland for setting fire to a Gulf Oil installation in Rotterdam in March, 1971. She had come into contact with members of the PFLP through her involvement in the French radical Left.

On August 5, 1971, the Moroccan sisters and Evelyn Barage received prison sentences ranging from ten to fourteen years. During their trial they admitted planning to blow up nine hotels in Israel on behalf of Fatah and the PFLP.

Also arrested with the girls was an elderly French couple, Pierre and Edith Bourghalter, who were paid by the PFLP to smuggle detonators hidden in a transistor radio. The couple was to contact the girls in Tel Aviv and pass them the detonators. The Bourghalters pleaded not guilty and have been held for a separate trial.

In the case of the girls their motives seem to have resulted from their political and emotional commitment to the fedayeen movement. Friendship with young Palestinians living in London and Paris appeared to be the

decisive factor in persuading them to embark on such a reckless adventure.

In the fall of 1971, two girls were arrested in Israel by security police after they were caught trying to bring suitcases laden with explosives through Israeli customs.

Convinced that the girls were innocent, the police brought them before the press to describe how they had been duped. One girl, introduced only as a 19-year-old Dutch citizen nicknamed Yeti, said she had met a Palestinian among a group of young people in Belgrade, Yugoslavia during summer holidays. "I was interested in the Arab," she told a press conference, "because he came from Beirut and we figured he had hashish. He did, and after smoking it together we became friends."

She described how the young Palestinian asked her as a favor to travel to Israel to deliver some clothes to relatives there. He told Yeti that his relatives in Bethlehem would give her $2000 to bring to him, and she would receive part of the sum when she returned to Europe. She was urged to take one of El Al's new 747 jumbo jets by her Palestinian friend who praised the Israeli airline as the "most modern and safest." According to Israeli security police, the brown leatherette case Yeti was given had a false bottom holding a bomb consisting of two explosive bricks and a detonation fuse. Israeli officials have suppressed details of how Yeti was discovered, but apparently she was intended as a live bomb and would have been blown up with the plane.

The second girl beguiled into carrying explosives aboard an El Al plane was a Peruvian seamstress identified only as Daliah. She told of a whirlwind romance with a young Palestinian engineer that took her throughout Latin America and to several European countries. The Arab proposed that they travel to Israel to be married at his home and he sent Daliah on ahead by El Al, promising that his parents and other relatives would meet her at Tel Aviv airport. He gave her two red suitcases containing false bottoms and presumably Daliah, too, was meant to serve as the instrument of a fedayeen attack on an Israeli plane. The suitcases were also discovered in an undisclosed manner.

Neither girl knew she was carrying explosives, according to an Israeli police spokesman. Yeti took off from London, but not on a jumbo jet, and Daliah left from Rome. After questioning in Israel both girls were freed and returned to Europe.

NOTES

1. Peter Snow and David Phillip, *Leila's Hijack War*, Pan Books, London, 1970.
2. Ibid. P. 175.

CHAPTER 10

Fact and Fantasy

Triumphant fedayeen reports of battles and raids against the Israeli enemy are reminiscent of tales from "The Arabian Nights." Exaggerated and distorted accounts of fighting are the trademarks of all Palestinian terrorist groups and they compete fiercely with each other in fashioning ever-more grandiose communiques boasting of imaginary victories, fictitious Israeli losses, and non-existent battles.

Students of Arab psychology frequently cite the Arab tendency to view reality through a special prism that focuses exclusively on the positive aspects of a situation. As one Western observer put it: "The Arab is inclined to believe what he wants to believe and not what the facts dictate he should believe."

The fecund oriental imagination and disregard for objective facts is at once a therapy and tragedy for the Arabs. Dramatic press and radio accounts of fedayeen prowess provide psychological relief for the Arab masses who have experienced the bitterness and shame of defeat by Israel time after time. To the refugees living without hope in the squalor of camps, fedayeen boasts stimulate injured Arab pride and fuel the emotions of a volatile and imaginative people.

Fedayeen information offices listen to Israeli broadcasts and are quick to claim credit for naturally caused mishaps such as personal tragedies and road accidents. During the summer of 1968, an Israeli youth with the surname Dayan drowned. Fatah hurriedly announced that one of its units had succeeded in killing the son of Israel's Minister of Defense, Moshe Dayan, while attacking his house. When Premier Levi Eshkol died of a heart attack, Fatah claimed it had helped kill him by firing Katyusha rockets at Kibbutz Degania. Eshkol, a founder of the Jordan valley settlement, occasionally visited Degania and this fact was enough to link the rocket harassment with the Premier's death. Perhaps one of the most publicized fedayeen claims involved an accident in which Moshe Dayan was seriously injured. The Defense Minister, an avid part-time archeologist, was participating in a dig near Tel Aviv in March, 1968. A large mound of earth suddenly shifted and trapped him. Thanks to the Israeli habit of gathering wherever the popular war hero makes an appearance, rescuers were immediately alerted and Dayan was rapidly extricated from the cave-in and treated for broken ribs and back injuries. The event was well documented in the international press. The day after the incident Fatah broadcast its own version. Communique #106 stated: "On the 20th of March the car of Moshe Dayan was ambushed. The automobile was damaged and rolled to the side of the road. In addition two escort cars were destroyed. Our forces escaped unscathed."

The fedayeen found a receptive Arab audience after the Six-Day War because of the prevailing mood of discouragement and despair. They adopted the Nazi philosophy of propaganda which utilized the "big lie" technique and postulates that no matter how grandiose or absurd a lie, if it is repeated loudly and frequently the masses will always retain something of the assertions.

One of Fatah's leaders, currently in an Israeli prison, was asked to comment on his organization's policy of reporting. He replied: "Try to understand. What's important is not what people actually perceive but the appearance of things. Israel announces that she has killed a certain number of terrorists and we claim we have killed scores of Israelis. The average Arab is confused as it is. The truth here is not important but rather the impression received from the announcements."

The fedayeen organizations have often misled foreign correspondents who were under the impression they were observing actual operations when in reality they had never crossed the cease-fire lines. Some journalists have devoted considerable coverage to fedayeen training centers, interviews with fedayeen leaders and descriptions of individual terrorists. The resulting feature stories, magazine spreads and dispatches become a kind of mirror image for the fedayeen and when they see photos of themselves in fierce, war-like poses and read the passionate utterances of their spokesmen they are actually persuaded they are achieving their goals. When a fantatic

Palestinian saboteur tells an American reporter: "We'll meet in Tel Aviv!" and then sees his words reproduced in a glossy, mass-circulation magazine he is deluded into thinking that he will some day really conquer Tel Aviv.

On some occasions foreign newsmen have witnessed actual fedayeen raids with rather unpleasant results. A BBC correspondent was wounded during one such escapade and in March, 1970, two French journalists were almost killed when they accompanied a unit of Saiqah into the occupied Golan Heights for the purpose of laying mines and ambushing Israeli army patrols. Before carrying out their mission they encountered a lone Israeli lieutenant in a jeep. The Israeli officer held the fedayeen at bay with a submachine gun while he radioed for help. A nearby Israeli tank unit moved quickly into the area and two of the terrorists were captured while the remaining thirteen, including the journalists, fled under cover of dusk. The next day Israeli units combing the area found telephoto lenses and other photographic equipment apparently dropped by the fleeing reporters.

In the Arab world the word often substitutes for the deed and the act of declaring an act is as meaningful as actually performing the act. Arab writers and thinkers are keenly aware of this lamentable tendency which is a basic reason for the Arab-Israeli impasse and the retarded social and political development of the Arab world.

The prestigious Egyptian newspaper, *Al Ahram*, commented on this Arab shortcoming in October, 1969: "When we Arabs loudly brag of an imaginary act we receive the same satisfaction that we would receive had we really performed the act."

In addition to contributing to the Mideast conflict by encouraging Israeli disdain for the Arabs, the baffling Arab proclivity to shape reality in accordance with self-deceiving fantasy also has disastrous consequences for the fedayeen. The lying creates an atmosphere of suspicion and disbelief among sophisticated Arabs. There have been cases of students, who, when joining Fatah, were told of atrocities perpetrated by the Israelis in Arab occupied zones. When the recruits discovered they had been misled they refused to carry out orders.

What is surprising is that the countries of the Communist bloc, particularly the Soviet Union and Communist China, often accept the distorted fedayeen reports and for propaganda purposes add their own ideological nuances and coloring to the communiques. Even Western newspapers have on occasion reported fedayeen boasts as facts. Although for a long time Israel would routinely issue denials following fedayeen communiques, this practice was eventually stopped since it was felt that the denials encouraged the fedayeen falsifications and when published were only carried as short follow items to the main story of the fedayeen claim.

According to Israeli military analysts, a major cause of heavy Arab losses is the inability of Arab soldiers to accurately assess and report battlefield conditions. The Arab fighter has not been trained to relay back to his command post exactly what he sees. All too often he reports what he thinks his commanding officer wants to hear. The fedayeen are the same as the Arab regulars in this respect and their reports either omit important facts or are fabrications based on wishful fantasies. A vivid and tragic example of this tendency occurred at the beginning of the Six-Day War when the destruction of Egypt's entire air force by Israeli jets was concealed by the Egyptian general staff from President Nasser for a whole day.

Lacking correct appraisals of battle conditions and

the lay of the land, the fedayeen are doomed to an inordinately high casualty rate. The low-ranking Arab officer, whether in the regular army or the ranks of the fedayeen, knows that the orders given to him are based on lies which in all probability he is in large measure responsible for. Knowing this, he will naturally doubt the logic of orders and will avoid taking unnecessary risks. The lie usually originates with the low-echelon officer who sees that his false reports are eagerly accepted by his superiors. The lie then progresses up through the levels of command and is embellished along the way. At the highest level a "final revision" is made before the fabricated report is released.

An examination of a year's reports of fedayeen missions reveal that fully a third have no basis in fact whatever. Based on the interrogation of captured terrorists it appears that fedayeen raiders often just shoot in the air or throw away their explosives and then report: "mission accomplished."

Grandiose and inflated claims are beneficial for recruiting and fund-raising purposes. The Arab press, however, is not unmindful of the false reporting emanating from fedayeen headquarters and has commented on the phenomenon.

Mohammed Heykal, writing in *Al Ahram* in June, 1969, commented: "there is dissension in the ranks of the resistance organizations and some shed more ink than enemy blood."

Among Palestinian intellectuals the fedayeen exaggerations have been a cause of embarrassment. Lecturing in Beirut in March, 1969, Dr. Tsalah Al Daba, a member of the Palestinian National Committee, said: "The sum total of the missions reported by the fedayeen military units comes to 700, whereas in reality less than thirty actually took place. The danger exists that Arab information units will grasp these figures as a fig leaf to clothe the nakedness resulting from the 1967 debacle."

One Arab journalist succinctly summed up the dilemma of the fedayeen. Writing in the official Libyan newspaper, *Al Tora* in April, 1970, on the inflated report of the Palestine Armed Struggle Command summmarizing the actions from April, 1969, to April, 1970, Mahmud Al Nabua said:

> What's the use of exaggerating? If these figures are accurate they are proof of the enemy's weakness and the possibility of destroying him in less than a year. On the other hand, the stories may be a total figment of the imagination. This is the fedayeen who plays upon the emotions of the Arab masses, promising them a carnival in Tel Aviv. These stories contain excessive naïveté and superficiality and there is the danger that the Palestinian revolution will repeat the mistakes of the Arab governments prior to June, 1967.

The emphasis placed by the fedayeen on propaganda in the Arab world has also been extended to the Western world where the Palestinian issue often provides a convenient and effective instrument for mobilizing public sympathy on behalf of the Arab cause and combating pro-Israel sentiments on the part of politicians, writers, and people in positions of cultural and social influence.

Israel's victory in the Six-Day War and the subsequent occupation of Arab lands altered the image of Israel as a nation threatened with genocide by implacable Arab foes. For much of the world accustomed to viewing the Jews as hapless, if tenacious, victims of history's convulsions, the emergence of a strong, resourceful nation of Jews fiercely determined to survive was difficult to accept. Seeming helplessness had engendered sympathy but self-sufficiency and success alienated support. The sentimental fascination with the "underdog" brought about a shift in affection. Arab belligerence and the events of May, 1967 were obscured by a new political and emotional consciousness casting Israel in the role of an expansionist, aggressive, and "inflexible" power whose alleged intransigence was the chief obstacle to peace in the Middle East.

Advocates of this view realized that the Palestinian cause, particularly the suffering of refugees in squalid camps, had become a real and exploitable fact of Middle Eastern life, one that elicits sincere concern among millions of Americans and Europeans. The complicated historical events behind the present Palestinian crisis are not apparent to the casual observer and newspaper reader and as a result Arab propagandists and enemies of Israel have capitalized on a golden opportunity.

By distorting history and changing their message to suit various audiences Arab supporters have been able to invoke the cause of Palestine to score not insignificant gains in the ongoing Arab-Israel propaganda war. The emergence of the fedayeen and reports of their terrorism attracted world attention and a wave of newspaper and magazine articles "discovered" the Palestinians. Unless Palestinian claims are satisfied, some of these articles asserted, the fedayeen will go on committing terrorist acts and pursuing guerrilla war against Israel. Some of these writings gave the impression that the fedayeen groups were truly representative of Palestinians living in Jordan and Lebanon and that they also enjoyed the confidence and respect of Palestinians under Israeli occupation. A tendency on the part of some pro-Arab Western journalists to depict the fedayeen as the new hope of the Arabs—the vanguard of the Arab revolution—by exaggerating and publicizing certain social and educational aspects of the guerrillas' program encouraged the view that at last the Palestinians had found a way out of their dilemma. Here was a movement that would both galvanize and guide the displaced masses to a new society in a re-gained land.

A true picture of the fedayeen is difficult to arrive at through sporadic press reports and sensational magazine accounts. Nor can the absurdity and inconsistencies of the Palestine Liberation Organization's doctrine of a multinational, democratic Palestine where "Jews, Christians, and Moslems can live in harmony" be dealt with in brief television reports or acrimonious debates. Frequently Fatah and other fedayeen assertions are taken at face value by some Western correspondents.

The image of the fedayeen as a progressive political and social force ready to accommodate Jewish national aspirations by allowing the Jews to exist as a minority in a new Palestine suited the ideological requirements of the Left in America and Europe. Arab propagandists, aided by the New Left, shed the traditional Arab message of advocating the destruction of Israel and the casting of her people into the sea. The new look was that of the Palestine liberation movement. By emphasizing the liberation aspect of the Palestinian struggle new allies were won among both Jewish and non-Jewish leftists.

Soon after the Six-Day War, the Arab League revamped its entire operation to emphasize the Palestinian revolution. The new propaganda offensive insisted on Israel's illegitimacy and alleged that Zionism was a colonialist, imperialist, and racist movement which had misled the Jewish people and was responsible for expelling the Palestinians from their land and inflicting atrocities on the Arab people.

By separating Zionism and Judaism the pro-Arab groups found qualified support among a number of Jewish leftists. These included several prominent personalities such as Prof. Noam Chomsky of MIT and journalist I. F. Stone. Having decided that the key to Mideast peace was the equitable settlement of both Jewish and Palestinian national claims these men embarked on a campaign designed to show that American-Jewish support for Israel was immoral insofar as it bolstered an "exclusivist" Zionist state. Their consensus was that it was Israel's responsibility to make the necessary overtures to the Palestinians—terrorism and belligerence notwithstanding. I. F. Stone, who in 1948 had described how Palestinians had voluntarily left Palestine, now accused the Jews of "moral myopia" and pushed a favorite leftist line that backs self-determination for all peoples except the Jews and consistently calls upon the Jews to exist as some super-moral, self-sacrificing agents of a new world order. In essence, the Left celebrated the nationalistic revolutions of everyone but the Jews who had successfully realized their own liberation in Zionism.

Paul Jacobs, a California radical writer, tried to arrange a dialogue between Israeli leftists, who recognized the Palestinian entity, and members of the fedayeen groups. In his book, *Between the Rock and the Hard Place*,[1] Jacobs describes his abortive attempt and tells how he was able to find willing Israelis but could not find Palestinians ready to meet with Israelis who were on record as sympathetic to their cause. The disparity between the romanticization of the Palestinian Liberation Organization's propaganda in the West and their actual views as expressed in the Mideast was commented on by a leading Israeli champion of Palestinian rights, Professor J. L. Talmon of the Hebrew University. In a letter to the editor commenting on a symposium of Palestinian intellectuals that appeared in *Newsweek* magazine in May, 1970, Talmon wrote: "The preservation of the state of Israel is an absolute axiom to the most peace-loving and anti-annexationist Israeli intellectual; troubled though he be by the tragic clash of rights and the plight of refugees.

"Sweetly reasonable as the plea for a 'nonsectarian' Palestine state may sound in the columns of *Newsweek*, it is being blared out elsewhere as a solemn vow to 'annihilate' the Jewish state. No one should blame survivors of Auschwitz for not treating such threats as rhetoric."

The most fertile ground for anti-Zionist, pro-Palestinian propaganda were the college campuses where there were many activist and vocal students oriented toward the Left. Fedayeen publications such as *Free Palestine* and *Fatah*, which show the guerrillas as a liberation movement linked with other liberation movements, were widely distributed on many campuses. The Organization of Arab Students, as well as the leftist Foreign Students Association and the Moslem Students Organization, blithely ignored all inconsistencies and contradictions implicit in their position and urged the Left to view the people of Palestine as kindred brothers of the "oppressed" Vietnamese people. Thus, when once Arab students in the United States and Europe hailed from Egypt, Jordan, Saudi Arabia, and other countries, now they all say they are "Palestinian."

Palestine Weeks featuring speakers and films were held at many colleges and fund-raising for Fatah was carried on. A persistent theme of leftist Arab propaganda was the analogy they drew between Israel and Vietnam.

Israel is likened to the United States-backed South Vietnamese regime, which imposes its will on the downtrodden masses. The message is made quite clear in the following quote from a broadside distributed by a radical leftist, pro-Arab group calling itself "The Committee to Support Middle East Liberation:

> If you defend Vietnamese self-determination—
> If you defend black self-determination—
> You must defend Arab self-determination.
> —It is the same struggle.

By continually labeling Israelis racists and the Palestinians progressives a scenario was developed whereby Israel was always synonymous with the wrong side and the Arabs with the right side. The armed struggle of the fedayeen was exploited to full advantage.

Many of the largely middle class, radical European, and American New Left youth, hungry for real experience and intoxicated on visions of bloody revolution à la Che Guevara and Frantz Fanon were inspired by Fatah's guerrilla war.

In Europe, the radical Left responded sympathetically to Arab propaganda linking the Palestinians to other "Third-World struggles." In France, Fatah replaced the Vietcong as the Number One liberation group at many French universities and secondary schools. A network of Vietnam Committees, which for years organized and led anti-American agitation among French intellectuals, was officially transformed into Palestine Committees at a number of French schools. At Nanterre, a hotbed of student dissidence, there were clashes between pro-Arab factions and Jewish youths and at several universities the walls were plastered with pro-Fatah slogans. During the

Paris riots in May, 1968, Jewish students arranged for a showing of the film *Exodus.* Students attending the screening were asked to pay a voluntary admission fee. At the end of the film, the students who had organized the screening announced that the proceeds would be donated to Fatah.

In England, student revolutionaries joined forces with representatives of the Fedayeen to organize a new group known as the Palestine Solidarity Campaign. The leftist campaign is active at several universities and shares facilities with the 6000-member General Union of Arab Students in Britain and distributes the English-language P.L.O. newspaper, *Free Palestine.* A leader of the group is Ghaif Armanshzi, the son of a former Syrian ambassador in London. He has arranged for as many as one hundred students, mostly British but including other nationalities, to spend summer holidays at a fedayeen camp in Jordan.

The direct encounter between the young Western revolutionaries and the men of Fatah often backfires. When 140 radical Western students—including ten girls —from Europe and the United States were recruited secretly by leftist organizations to attend a one-month training and indoctrination program there were fears on the part of Western diplomats in Amman that Fatah was seeking to create its own Foreign Legion. There is evidence that Fatah as an organization receiving most of its funds from such right-wing traditionalist countries as Saudi Arabia and Kuwait was embarrassed by the extreme views of the foreign youth and was not enthusiastic about the program which had been promoted by propagandists abroad.

The young activists arrived in Amman in the summer of 1969. The announced purpose of the workshop was to acquaint foreign students with the Arab cause, so they could carry the fedayeen message back home. The students had looked forward to guerrilla training but instead spent their days listening to lectures on Middle Eastern history, politics, and Marxist ideology. Fatah leaders complained of the lack of discipline among the students because they defied fedayeen orders to stay out of sight and instead roamed through Amman's market places in search of souvenirs. For their part, the students were disappointed by Yasir Arafat's lack of ideological consistency. In one widely reported exchange, the Fatah leader angrily told a journalist who was badgering him with political questions, "I use Saudi money to buy weapons from Red China. Now what kind of ideology is that?"

The students' greatest disillusionment was the attitude of the rank and file Palestinians. Fundamentally religious and xenophobic, the Fatah men have little use for ideology and wish only to kill Jews and seize land. They were not ready to invite the full participation of foreigners in what they see as their holy war.

Newsweek magazine reported that in one refugee camp the students visited, several Jewish members of the group tried to explain to the Palestinians that their leftist ideology allowed them to view the Mideast situation "correctly" despite their ethnic background. The refugees were unconvinced and angrily tried to expel the students before they were restrained by Fatah tour guides. The students were disappointed by what they saw as the narrow scope of the Palestinian struggle and some sized up Arafat as a petty bourgeois. One American, who had left college to join the fight against Israel, admitted to a reporter that whenever he tried to discuss international revolution with the fedayeen "all they would say was *baladi, baladi*—my country, my country." The young man concluded, "Finally I got the message. In their eyes this was not my fight."

The success of the fedayeen propaganda among the student Left was encouraging to the anti-Israel camp and persuaded non-student circles that the Palestine struggle was the best theme available to the Arabs. An example of the Arab conversion to the Palestinian cause was the conference of the Association of Arab American University Graduates at Wayne State University in Detroit, Michigan in December, 1969. The theme of the three-day meeting was "The Palestinian Revolution—Its International, Social, and Technical Dimensions." Papers on such topics as Palestinian law and arts and Palestinians under occupation were read to a large gathering of Arab academics, pro-Arab sympathizers and members of Detroit's sizable Arab community—the largest in the United States with 40,000 residents of mainly Syrian and Lebanese origin and 5000 Palestinians. Speakers praised the fedayeen movement and called for more understanding of the Arab cause in the U.S. There was no question that the Palestinian liberation movement was projected as synonymous with the Arab cause and the absolute endorsement of the fedayeen in resolutions without any demurrer regarding Arab terrorism illustrated how thoroughly and effectively the Palestinian movement had taken over pro-Arab activities in the United States.

Although most of the propaganda activities on college campuses have been carried on by the Organization of Arab Students, comprising 1000 national members who pay $7.00 a year to the national organization, generous aid in the form of printed materials and speakers is furnished by the Arab Information Center in New York, the Palestine Liberation Organization and the staffs of Arab embassies. Funds from the Arab League are allocated to student propaganda activities. The student organization has confined its criticism of "reactionary" Arab regimes to discussions and forums involving the New Left. At its conventions the Arab students are careful to refrain from taking up resolutions that deal specifically with any Arab government. In this way the continued support of the rightist Arab regimes in the form of funds and materials is ensured while simultaneously the support of the militant Left is attracted by deploring the non-revolutionary, anti-progressive Arab regimes.

New Leftist youth organizations have varied in their commitment to the Palestinian cause. Some were willing to disseminate anti-Israel materials and pay lip service to the fedayeen while conserving their passion for the Vietnam issue. Others were persuaded that on the basis of Marxist analysis the Jewish State must be condemned as a tool of Western imperialism and the friend of the United States. Permanent committees on the Middle East were organized by the Maoist group, Youth Against War and Fascism, an extension of the Workers World Party, and the Trotskyite Young Socialist Alliance, the youth arm of the Socialist Workers Party.

Radical black organizations, primarily the Black Panthers, found the Palestinian issue a convenient means of exploiting anti-Semitic sentiment while disguisng it as "anti-Zionist," not "anti-Jewish." But as one black student leader put it, the Jewish community is seen as one of the most oppressive members of the "Establishment" and since Israel is "the darling of the Jewish community," attacking Israel "shakes up the establishment." Panther leaders Eldridge Cleaver, Huey Newton, Bobby Seale, and David Hilliard spoke out frequently in support of Fatah and linked Zionism with fascism and Israel with U.S. imperialism. Cartoons depicting Israel as an aggressor and Zionists as pigs have accompanied articles in Panther publications with headlines such as "Palestine Guerrillas vs. Israeli Pigs." The Black Panthers define Zionism as "kosher nationalism" and descriptions of "heroic" fedayeen exploits sometimes have been printed verbatim from Fatah publications. The Panthers have also formed close ties with Fatah, and Eldridge Cleaver, who lives in Algeria, has visited fedayeen camps and announced an agreement whereby Black Panther members would be trained in guerrilla warfare by Fatah. The strong anti-Israel line pursued by the Panthers has been muted lately in accordance with a general Panther strategy of toning down the group's violent image. The general disintegration of the movement has also relegated the Mideast question, never a main issue, to the realm of a minor consideration. Nevertheless, the Panthers' vicious Jew-baiting and venomous anti-Israel propaganda is a matter of record.

Joining the radical Left and the Black Panthers in propagandizing on behalf of the Palestinians is a small group of leftist anti-Zionists who identify themselves as "Jewish Radicals." Their existence helps the Arabs most by providing a kind of proof of the thesis that alleges a dichotomy between Judaism and Zionism. The most vocal and active of this latter group for a time was Arthur Waskow, a Washington-based political scientist who leads the National Jewish Organizing Project. Waskow is best known for his re-working of the traditional Passover ritual known as "The Freedom Seder." Both in its printed form and when produced in guerrilla-theater style Waskow's text condemns Israel as capitalistic, aggressive, and expansionist and attacks universal Jewish support for Zionism as immoral and reactionary. Waskow thinks it is Israel's duty to satisfy the Palestinians by creating the conditions for an autonomous Palestinian state. His views are formulated with little regard for the social and political realities of the Middle East. He ignores the absence of any conciliatory attitude on the part of the Palestinian Arabs.

The Middle East is not a major concern of the New Left and on most campuses only a small number of students are interested in the Palestine question. However, to the extent that the radical Left concerns itself with the Middle East, the Palestinians have gained a more receptive audience for their cause. By cleverly assessing the rhetoric and dogma of the Left, the Arab propagandists were successful in taking advantage of the New Left's affinity for the "third world" of national revolutions and international leftist solidarity. The impact of the Palestinian campaign in Europe, the United States, and Latin America has been felt mostly in the ranks of the most radical and authoritarian segment of the Left, since the democratic Left continued in its support for Israel. Israel's socialistic economic institutions and her progressive social attitudes appealed far more to the humanistic Left than the violence of the fedayeen and the aggressive and backward social structures of the so-called revolutionary Arab nations. This attitude was summed up in a statement issued by twenty representatives of the German Left, including the writers Günter Grass and Uwe Johnson:

> The lines are not drawn so simply that one can always automatically side with the Third World. Merely because the Arabs belong to the Third World, they are not yet ipso facto the purest of angels. The Israelis are the ones who are menaced; it is the Arabs, on the other hand, who are planning attack, expulsion, and annihilation. One must take

> sides, in the first instance, with progress, with justice, with humanity—rather than with a given group of nations. Just as from these ideas follows the stand we have taken against the United States and for the Vietnamese people, so too it follows that we must take a stand against Nasser and for Israel.

Of particular concern to Israel and Jews abroad was the participation in extremist groups by Jewish youth and the emergence of fringe anti-Zionist Jewish organizations. The appearance of self-hating Jews endorsing the ideology and aims of the Jewish people's enemy was not a new phenomenon in history. But the alienation of a large number of Jewish youths in varying degrees from Israel and the goals of Zionism in the post Six-Day War period pained older Jews whose consciousness was seared by memories of the Nazi holocaust and the rebirth of the Jewish people as exemplified by the establishment of Israel. In the minds of most Jews, Zionism is far from a chauvinistic movement determined to oppress the other peoples of Palestine. It is a movement of liberation and emancipation for the Jewish people, but only Jews conversant with their own history can fully appreciate this conviction. In the case of many European and American Jewish youth, their ignorance of the events that have led to today's Mideast crisis creates an attitude toward Israel that is uninformed and ambiguous.

Parents who staunchly supported Israel, neglected to educate their children in their beliefs and then were astonished when the young men and women revealed a lack of concern for Israel's destiny. Those Jewish students who felt sympathetic toward Israel and opposed the false dogma of the Left on the subject of the Mideast were at first startled by the Arab propaganda offensive and were ill-equipped to respond to attacks because they were not well-versed in Middle East history and thus were unable to argue against experienced Arab speakers. A real concern for the Palestinian refugees and a preoccupation with finding a just solution to the Mideast problem for both Jews and Palestinians further complicated the position of young Jews who had come to regard uncritical support for Israel as another middle-class value they scorned.

The post Six-Day War period saw changes in Israel's political atmosphere, and leftist Zionist students, uncomfortable with Israeli official policy which until recently denied the existence of a Palestinian entity, were encouraged by a growing movement in Israel that recognized the necessity of coming to terms with Palestinian national claims by expressing a readiness to negotiate a settlement providing for Palestinian territorial independence. In line with the new spirit of ad hoc affiliations and flexible groupings evident at many colleges, the American Zionist Youth Foundation, a coordinating agency, dissolved the national Student Zionist Organization and gave support to individual campus units of students who were pro-Israel. Some were leftist in orientation, others were Zionist in a more conventional sense, and at some relatively unpoliticized colleges the groupings were simply based on Jewish identity and favorable sentiments toward Israel.

A new Jewish consciousness of the Palestinian question was expressed in many articles appearing in campus newspapers published by Jewish students and figured prominently in symposiums and debates. Activist Jewish students protested the attitudes and actions of Arab governments and demonstrated against fedayeen terrorism, attacks on and the hijacking of El Al planes, the treatment of Jews in Arab countries, and the anti-Israel, anti-Jewish policies of the Soviet Union. Pro-fedayeen advocates were challenged on the grounds of the inconsistencies of the Palestine liberation movement's doctrine and the criminal violence of the guerrillas. The activities of the pro-Israeli counter-propaganda effort brought to the fore the extent of the debate among Jews concerning Palestine and an equitable solution of the essential Mideast conflict.

In addition to the intensive Arab propaganda effort on campus and among the followers of the New Left special attention was directed to organized American Christianity. The new image of the fedayeen as a constructive social force prepared to concede the Jews a form of existence as a minority in a new Palestinian state attracted the interest of several American churchmen who felt that the ostensible fedayeen program offered a way out of the Mideast impasse. Just as it has divided the Left, the Mideast controversy has sparked an intense debate among both Protestants and Catholics. The identification of the Jewish people with the land of Israel and the significance of Israel in Christian theology has led to strong feelings on both sides of the issue. Pro-Arab churchmen have sought to take advantage of the humanitarian aspects of the Palestinian problem to push anti-Israel resolutions at church councils and conferences. They moved quickly after the Six-Day War to bring about a change in church attitudes toward Israel and heavily emphasized a distinction between Zionism and Judaism in order to assuage the misgivings of clergymen who suspected that opposition to Israel was uncomfortably close to anti-Semitism. In several Protestant sects sympathy for the Arab cause, especially when couched in terms of the Palestinians, was motivated by substantial church investments in missionary activity in Arab lands. Organized in the form of missionary fellowships, Protestant groups collect money in the United States to support schools and proselytizing activities in Arab countries. Such well-known educational institutions as the American University in Beirut, where many fedayeen leaders studied and where pro-fedayeen indoctrination is openly carried on, are directly supported by American Protestants. Some churchmen have been responsive to Palestinian propaganda because they feel the minority Christian communities in Arab countries would suffer if it appeared that the U.S. churches were sympathetic toward Israel.

Of the estimated $10 million spent by the Arab League on propaganda in the United States and Europe since 1967, a considerable portion has gone to setting up pro-Arab organizations and pressure groups with the backing of Protestant and Catholic clergymen. The Arab propagandists and their supporters employ theological anti-Semitism as well as anti-Zionism in their political struggle against Israel. The anti-Semitic materials range from sophisticated theological arguments to the revival of crude medieval blood libels and Nazi propaganda against the Jews. American Protestant and Orthodox clergymen operating out of Beirut and New York have distributed a master strategy plan to Christian leaders and seminarians throughout the United States for the purpose of countering Christian popular support of Israel. The strategy includes an appeal to Christian leaders to "seek cooperation with existing pro-Arab groups in the United States," and a call to "organize boycotts of tours to the Holy Land." A campaign was organized by several Protestant clergymen in the U.S. to bring the Arab situation to the attention of Congress and to sway American public opinion through letters to the editor and the distribution of pro-Arab literature and films. An indication of the size of the Arab church effort is a report in the Lebanese newspaper *Al Hayat*, which states that Metropolitan Philip Saliba, Archbishop of the Syrian Antiochian Orthodox Archdiocese of New York and North America, visited Beirut in June, 1968, and urged Arab nations to double their contributions for propaganda to "not less than $20 million to establish information centers in the United States."

The American Friends Service Committee, a Quaker group, took a special interest in the Mideast impasse and in lobbying activities. It promoted a study of the Mideast situation which concluded that Israel was unduly "inflexible" in insisting on face-to-face negotiations with the Arabs concerning future Mideast boundaries. The Friends decided that Israel's policies were hard-line and "rigid" and supported this opinion by falsely construing Israel's desire for "secure" frontiers as tantamount to annexationism. The Quaker group further played into Arab propagandists' hands by maintaining that the plight of the Arab refugees "has been inadequately reported," yet the Friends' study, "Search For Peace In The Middle East," in its original form made no mention of the Jewish refugees from Arab countries.

It is the view of Rabbi Marc Tanenbaum of the American Jewish Committee, an expert on Jewish-Christian relations, that despite the campaign to promote the fedayeen movement among American Christians, the terrorism of the extremists tends to frighten off much Christian support which is reluctant to endorse a movement that hijacks airplanes and blows up school buses. Tanenbaum says that much liberal Protestant opinion has shifted from a previously "critical position toward Israel to a more sympathetic and even-handed understanding." And he points out that both conservative Roman Catholic and Protestant opinion "has shown an increased commitment to Israel's needs." The American Jewish Committee says that by early 1970 a clear recognition by Christian writers that Israel is no myth and really exists had emerged and the organization quoted the Rev. John Sheerin, editor of the Paulist publication, *The Catholic World*, as saying that Israel's existence "is every bit as valid as that of numerous other states whose legality is never questioned."

The idea that Israel exists illegitimately has been stressed by Palestinian propagandists wherever they have been active. Spanish-speaking America has been the scene of intensive pro-Arab activity and fedayeen representatives have sought an alliance with revolutionary guerrilla groups. As elsewhere, the issue of the Middle East has split the Left and elements of the Catholic Church in Latin America. Arab propaganda in Latin America, where its tone is virulently anti-Semitic, has been rebuffed by such prominent members of the progressive Catholic hierarchy as Sergio Mendez-Arceo, Bishop of Cuernavaca, Mexico, who has spoken out frequently and eloquently against anti-Semitism and in favor of Israel.

In Canada the attempt of Arab propagandists to disclaim a relationship between anti-Zionism and anti-Semitism was refuted by Dr. Alan T. Davies, a leading Canadian theological writer who pointed out in the August, 1970, issue of *The Christian Century* that "to much of the Jewish community anti-Zionism and anti-Semitism, if not exactly identical, are much less disparate than may appear to the superficial observer. Anti-Zionism sooner or later reveals a distressing tendency to shade into anti-Semitism. . . . Not many Jews take the position that Israel, by definition, is beyond reproach. Nevertheless, if I read the Jewish mind correctly, not many Jews are prepared to accept a definition of Zionism which interprets it as a heresy or as an aberration within Judaism. . . . Zionism, as an affirmation of Jewish existence interwoven with the unique attachment of Judaism to Eretz Israel for profound reasons of history, cannot be called a heresy. Given this reality, it is exceedingly difficult on the emotional level for the victims of holocaust to distinguish anti-Zionism from anti-Semitism, however clear the distinction may seem to gentiles. This is especially the case when Jews read anti-Zionist literature that is cast in the same language and utilizes the same images as classical anti-Semitism."

The black radical anti-Israel propaganda was countered by public statements denouncing fedayeen terrorism and endorsing Israel's insistence on direct negotiations with the Arabs which have been issued by leading Negro political and civil rights figures, including Bayard Rustin, Mayor Richard Hatcher of Gary, Indiana, Congresswoman Shirley Chisholm of New York, Roy Wilkins, and Roy Innis. Several black journalists visited Israel and their reports indicated a generally favorable and sympathetic attitude toward Israel's handling of the occupation and her behavior toward the Arab minority. Bayard Rustin, an expert on American Negro affairs, has pointed out in an interview that blacks are on the whole not anti-Semitic and certainly do not see any natural community of interest with the Palestinian extremists.

NOTE

1. Random House, New York, 1970.

CHAPTER 11

Fedayeen in Prison

The number of men and women Palestinian terror-ists held in Israeli jails fluctuates constantly. As of November, 1970, Israel's nine jails held approximately 3000 fedayeen. Of this total 1500, including sixty-five women, had been convicted by Israeli courts; 1000 were awaiting trial and 500 had been detained temporarily by administrative order. Of the 1500 convicted fedayeen 200, among them five women, were serving sentences of life imprisonment and 600 had been sentenced to terms longer than five years.

Because Israel's prison facilities are not large enough to accommodate all convicted fedayeen some are freed from time to time before serving their full sentences on condition that they pledge to refrain from terrorism and sever all ties with fedayeen organizations. Some Arabs are released in return for their promise that they will leave Israel. In most cases these pledges are kept.

The following account is based on a series of interviews with fedayeen prisoners in the summer of 1970.

The women prisoners were silent as the Israeli visitor entered their cell. Only one of the four nodded her head in a silent greeting. All the girls were dark-haired, attractive, and in their twenties. The room was immaculate. The warden, Miss Raya Epstein, said, "The cleanest and best-looking prisoners are the Arab girls. The Jewish prisoners are here for criminal offenses and many of them are prostitutes. Many of the Arab girls, on the other hand, are the elite of West Bank Arab society. Most of them come from prosperous and respectable families. They're from the intelligentsia, graduates of university or teachers' colleges."

The walls were bare except for a huge poster of Che Guevara. Miriam Sharshir, a pretty 20-year-old sentenced to life imprisonment, explained, "We love Che. He urged war against imperialism everywhere."

Miriam, a member of the Popular Front for the Liberation of Palestine, was convicted of placing a bomb in the cafeteria at the Hebrew University in March, 1969. Twenty-nine students were injured in the explosion.

In one corner of the room a delicate-looking girl was reading what she said was a book on philosophy. Her name was Auda Rashmiya and she was serving a life term for participating in the blowing up of a supermarket in Jerusalem in which two persons were killed and nine civilians injured. Her appearance suggested a gentle young woman, but the warden said later that during an outburst of anger Auda had beaten a guard so badly that the latter had to be hospitalized. Auda, twenty-three, the daughter of a Moslem family, was born in Jerusalem but grew up in Ramallah. She had completed one year as a student of philosophy at Beirut University when the Six-Day War broke out. In December, 1967, she decided to return to her parents' home in Ramallah. Although reluctant to discuss her political affiliations before the Six-Day War, Auda says that after June, 1967, she joined the PFLP. Why the Habash group and not Fatah? she was asked.

"All of the organizations have an identical goal," she replied and refused to discuss the ideological and tactical differences separating the various fedayeen groups.

"Wouldn't it have been better to finish your studies in Beirut instead of blowing up a supermarket?" the visitor asked.

"My nation is under the yoke of imperialism and in such circumstances it is natural for me to be here," she answered excitedly. And then, after speaking proudly of how she had been sentenced to life imprisonment on three counts, Auda asked if the visitor could help influence the authorities to separate the Arab prisoners from the Jews. "We are political prisoners," she asserted.

Raya Epstein, the warden, who had been listening quietly interjected, "You are criminals. You killed innocent civilians. Doesn't your conscience bother you occasionally for blowing up a civilian store? Most of the customers were women; you could have easily killed mothers and children."

Auda replied in equally angry tones: "I am not guilty. You caused this. And as for women and children—in your country everyone serves in the army, including women. There is no difference between soldiers and civilians. The children are also legitimate targets for they will grow up and become soldiers. You have not been any better than us. Before 1948 Jews used to blow up Arab marketplaces. I read this myself. Today we have no choice. I'm not happy killing people, but there is no other way."

"Do you look forward to the day when there will be peace between Israel and the Arabs?" the visitor then asked.

"Peace?" Auda asked. "Only if you return to the countries you came from."

A few days earlier some of the Arab women prisoners were in Hebrew class when one of them suddenly asked their teacher where she was born.

"France," said the teacher.

"Then why don't you return there and tell your parents to go back where they came from?" one fedayeen girl suggested.

The teacher responded: "Their last address before coming to Israel was Auschwitz."

The passionate beliefs and fanatic devotion of the women fedayeen have not lessened behind bars. Some have even developed a more intense hatred of Israel. The only woman prisoner ready to express regrets over her past actions is Fatma Barnavai, the first female terrorist arrested and imprisoned for life after the Six-Day War. In October, 1967, Fatma was one of a group of Fatah members who attempted to dynamite the Zion Cinema in Jerusalem. The explosives were detected before detonation when the commander of Fatah in Jerusalem was caught. He gave Israeli intelligence the names of several accomplices. Among these names were Fatma's and that of her sister, Ihsan, who escaped to Jordan.

Fatma, whose father is a Nigerian Moslem who emigrated to Palestine and married an Arab woman, has turned into a model prisoner, friendly, well-liked and much praised by guards and warden. She is the only Arab prisoner willing to share a cell with a Jewish inmate and, according to the warden, is a great help to her cell mate, a young drug addict.

Fatma had this to say about herself: "I am a native of Jerusalem where I completed my schooling and became a registered nurse. I left Jordan to work in Saudi Arabia, but I soon became discouraged. I was saving money, but the terrible heat and tough working conditions got me down and I decided to come back to Palestine. I worked in a hospital in Kalkilya in Jordan and was there when the Six-Day War broke out. I was shocked by what happened.

"I wasn't a member of Fatah, I joined them by chance. I came to Jerusalem, to my sister Ihsan. Her boyfriend was a member of Fatah. His name is Shauki Shihrur and he persuaded us to plant a bomb in the cinema. I didn't think much of it. What I did I did because of what happened at Kalkilya during the Six-Day War. They didn't force me to take part, but they told me the bomb was harmless, that it would only make a loud noise and frighten people.

"The three of us—myself, Ihsan, and Shauki—went to the theater. I carried the bomb in my briefcase and left it under some seats. Later, I left with Ihsan and Shauki followed us after a short interval. We heard explosions and Ihsan and I couldn't sleep that night for fear that many people had been killed in the cinema. We later found out that the bomb was discovered and detonated in the street.

"I'm happy it didn't explode in the theater. Now I look to the future and hope everything will turn out all right for me."

The number of Arab women terrorists in Israel's

Naveh Tirza central women's prison has never amounted to more than forty at any given time. Israeli policy is to free women prisoners whenever possible after they have served a portion of their sentence. In many cases the women terrorists are as dangerous, if not more so, as the men but in an effort to assuage Arab sensibilities it has been decided to adopt a more lenient approach toward women offenders.

Israel spends approximately $300 a month on the upkeep of each woman prisoner, approximately twice as much as is spent on their male counterparts. Maintaining services for a smaller number of inmates necessitates the greater expense.

For many of the prisoners their first encounters with Israelis occur while in jail and they sometimes develop a curiosity about life in the Jewish state. Prior to their capture they knew very little of Israel since in most Arab countries anything Israeli is taboo and no mention is made of Israel except in virulent propaganda.

Most of the women prisoners study Hebrew and their teacher is impressed with their application. Gradually an interest emerges in Jewish history, traditions and customs and the prisoners are surprised to learn that Israelis learn about the Arabs in their schools. Several prisoners have discovered modern Hebrew poetry. One Arab girl studied Hebrew poetry and at a ceremony marking the end of the school year analyzed a poem by Israel's national poet, Haim Nahman Bialik, for her sister fedayeen students.

"We have taken pains to stimulate their intellectual appetite," Miss Epstein says in describing the interest that some of the women show in taking part in the celebrations of Jewish holidays. There have been, however, instances when the fedayeen display determined resistance to learning about Jewish culture. Miss Epstein said most demonstrations are limited to token protests involving specific demands such as insisting on doing only agricultural work in order "to feel the earth of our homeland."

Sometimes close, friendly relations develop between the prisoners and their warders. Several women have kept in touch with Miss Epstein after their release and one has been a guest in the warden's home.

The liberal attitude is taken for granted by most prisoners and such services as psychiatric counseling are accepted as their due. "You're winning, you can afford to be magnanimous," one prisoner said.

Miss Epstein and other Israeli penologists are convinced that the humane, liberal approach will bear fruit one day and that it will help to dull the edge of Arab hatred and resentment.

The daily routine is neither overly arduous nor punishing for the women. They arise at 5:45 A.M., wash, dress, eat breakfast, and report for work by 7:30 A.M. They work until 2:00 P.M. (those engaged in farming work until twelve noon). Many of the women work fewer hours because they study and school is held in the morning instead of the afternoon at the suggestion of the teacher. The female prisoners have free time in the afternoon. After six they are allowed to watch television for two hours (three hours on Fridays).

The Arab male prisoner is treated with far more rigidity than the women but the general conditions are humane. The men are not severely punished and also enjoy the benefits of a liberal prison administration. Once accustomed to humane treatment, the male inmates begin demanding rights and privileges and are convinced that the rules of the game oblige Israel, the victor, to treat Arab prisoners kindly whereas the Arabs, whose cause in their eyes is the just one, are entitled to mistreat Israeli prisoners in their jails and Jewish citizens in their countries.

Fedayeen complaints in jail are few. Prisoners in one jail held a hunger strike to protest against not being supplied with Arab-language periodicals. A frequent complaint is that they are not being given enough fresh fruit. In response the authorities permitted prisoners' families to bring two pounds of fruit when visiting. But it was soon discovered that the fruit was used to smuggle forbidden items, such as drugs and weapons. Now inmates can purchase fruit and other supplementary foods at prison canteens with money their relatives send them. An International Red Cross representative has told the Israeli authorities that his organization was satisfied the prisoners are well-fed despite the latter's allegations. In the dining room the day's menu is posted in Arabic and usually offers bread, margarine, jam, olives, and powdered milk for breakfast; meat or fish, rice, soup, and vegetables for lunch and bread, cheese, tea, and tomatoes for supper. The daily caloric intake amounts to 2800. The cost of housing and feeding a Palestinian terrorist amounts to $1700 a year, more than social welfare cases in Israel receive.

Often the general Israeli public is astounded to learn the extent of fedayeen prisoners' privileges. They live apart from the Jewish prisoners but their respective conditions are similar. The Jewish convicts are allowed two family visits a month while the terrorists are permitted to see relatives once a month. The same guards are used for both categories of prisoners.

Elias Dernitzer, warden of the Ramleh jail, where many long-term Arab prisoners are held, said in an interview: "I wish every citizen of Israel received as good medical care as the Arab prisoners do, including psychiatric treatment. Just the other day a prisoner was returned to us after receiving special treatment for three months in an Israeli mental hospital. We don't do this for gratitude but because it's our job. I also think these measures are well worth the effort."

Dernitzer denied Arab allegations that prisoners were beaten and recalled the following incident to support his denial. The mother of one of the Arabs in Ramleh jail came from Amman and demanded to see the warden. She said she had heard in Jordan that her son and other fedayeen were being beaten. Dernitzer called the woman's son into his office and there in front of his mother he confirmed that there was no mistreatment or torture carried on in the institution. When saying goodbye to the warden, the woman from Amman said, "I now know the rumors about beating were spread by a recently freed prisoner who returned to Jordan. I now understand that he had to describe Israeli prison conditions as intolerable in order to show his bravery."

The excellent medical care, substantial food, and good sanitary conditions of the jails, including abundant hot water, provide most of the Arab prisoners with a higher standard of living than they enjoyed on the outside. Many of them concede this.

Unlike most of the women prisoners, the Arab men display apathy while in jail despite the fedayeen ideology supposedly motivating them. One gets the impression that some of them are actually satisfied that their time of actual fighting is over and that they have found a kind of refuge behind bars. In contrast to the resistance and guerrilla fighters of Europe during World War II, the convicted fedayeen are not alert and do not attempt to escape. In this respect they resemble Arab soldiers taken as prisoners during the Sinai campaign in 1956 and the Six-

Day War. Although thousands were imprisoned temporarily there was not one attempt to escape.

Members of Fatah are put together with members of other fedayeen groups and rivalries develop. One result is that the Arabs frequently inform on one other. Ramleh prison warden Dernitzer says he always knows exactly what is going on in the jail without making any special effort.

Frequently there are discrepancies between what the fedayeen say for public consumption and what they are willing to say in private. One terrorist was brought to trial on charges of attempting to blow up a factory in Nazareth. When asked in court if he repented his action he replied that he was only sorry he had failed. Later in jail, he told the warden to disregard what he had said at the trial. "That's an entirely different thing," he explained, "here I will be obedient."

An Israeli Arab named Nimar Fawzi was sentenced to life imprisonment for dynamiting two apartment buildings in Haifa and causing the death of two elderly civilians. He was asked why he had used such abusive language during the trial. "I knew I would get life in any event," he replied. "I had to speak that way; here it is another matter. I hope for peace between Jews and Arabs."

Israeli prison authorities are convinced the fedayeen prefer strong discipline. This gives them an excuse for not risking punishment by rebelling. Most of the male fedayeen spend their prison years in idleness. There is no instinct or drive for self-improvement. The educated prisoners keep to themselves, avoiding contact with the lower-class Arabs who form the majority. There are few signs of camaraderie or group purpose.

The small number of violations of prison regulations

consist mainly of insulting guards. Offenders are punished by having visiting and mail privileges revoked for varying periods.

The first member of Fatah captured and jailed in Israel is Mahmoud Hijazi. He was wounded in January, 1965, after infiltrating from Jordan and unsuccessfully trying to destroy an irrigation installation at an Israeli border settlement. His trial attracted a good deal of attention, partly because an Algerian lawyer who flew to Israel to defend Hijazi was refused permission to enter the country. Hijazi pleaded guilty to charges of attempted sabotage and illegal possession of a weapon and was sentenced to death by a military court—the first death sentence in Israel since the trial of Nazi war criminal Adolf Eichmann in 1961. The punishment was revoked in 1966 and a second trial resulted in a prison term of thirty years. In February, 1971, Hijazi was exchanged for Shmuel Rosenwasser, the Israeli watchman kidnapped by fedayeen near the Lebanese border in January, 1970.

Hijazi became a kind of folk hero among the fedayeen and many of the Arabs, despite the fact that he had joined Fatah for mercenary reasons and had been dishonorably discharged from the Jordanian army. At the time of the interview Hijazi was thirty-two, but he looked older. His hair was going gray and his face was pale. He said he felt weak and was troubled by a stomach ulcer as well as weak kidneys and a skin ailment on his legs. When he was captured he was seriously wounded and survived an intestinal hemorrhage after surgery and many blood transfusions.

At the time of the interview he had just been released from punishment in solitary confinement for a disciplinary violation. He had learned Hebrew in jail and spoke it well. He was generally cautious in his replies:

Question: Did you expect to serve a long sentence in jail when you were caught?

Answer: I thought at the time I would stay in prison at least five years and then would go free. Of course I didn't know at the time that war would break out.

Q: But you and your Fatah comrades wanted war. Only it turned out differently than you imagined.

A: My comrades, [said with an ironic smile] I don't believe any more in friends. I've learned that you can only trust yourself. It's true, the war did not have good results. The only thing I gained was that my family, which lives in Jericho [on the West Bank], can now visit me.

Q: Are you proud of the honors you have been given as the first member of Fatah to be captured by Israel?

A: Yes I was honored, especially by Fatah. But I have paid for these honors.

Q: Would you do what you did if you had these years to live over?

A: It's impossible to reverse the flow of time, but I do see things differently now. I have changed a great deal and I read the Koran. I have a lot of time to think.

Q: Do you see any possibility of peace between Israel and the Arabs in the near future?

A: I do not see the possibility of a compromise solution. What has Israel done for peace? For the refugees? I see only war in the future.

Q: But you haven't gained anything from war in the past.

A: Yes, you're right. We made you [Israel] stronger, we caused you to be good fighters because of our fatuous words and empty talk. We have lost three wars. Maybe we will lose the next one too. But you will get only one chance to lose a war.

Q: Have you learned anything from your contacts with Israelis?

A: As a child in Jerusalem I knew few Jewish youths. Now they are living near me. I see that they are regular people without horns and tails. There are good ones and bad ones.

Q: How do you envision your future?

A: I shall certainly be in jail another five years.

Q: If they release you where will you go?

A: I will go to Jerusalem. That is my city. I love Jerusalem. I'll be able to set myself up again. Before the war money was raised on my behalf. They told me a sum equivalent to 20,000 Israel pounds ($4,770) is on deposit in my name in an Amman bank.

Q: Would you be surprised if there was peace between Israel and the Arabs?

A: The Arabs are afraid of peace. They know the Jews are intelligent. What they have not taken from us in war they will take in peace. All fear peace with Israel. This would not be a real peace. I just don't trust Jews.

Another convicted fedayeen interviewed was William Nasser, the former deputy Fatah commander in Jerusalem. Nasser, whose mother is Jewish and whose father is a Christian Arab, was arrested in 1968 and charged with several terrorist actions. Nasser stood trial together with the former Fatah commander in Jerusalem, Kamel Nimri, whose mother is also Jewish. It was Nasser who turned Nimri over to Israeli intelligence. Nimri in turn informed on several fedayeen. Both Nimri and Nasser are now serving life sentences.

Nasser, a handsome man of twenty-five, studied in Lebanon and Spain before the Six-Day War. He says he joined Fatah as a student in 1965 and was selected to join the first group that went to Communist China for training in sabotage and guerrilla warfare. After the trip to China he returned to Jordan where he met Nimri. They were both assigned to setting up a Fatah network in the Jerusalem area. Nasser agreed to answer several questions.

Q: Does the fact that your mother is Jewish account somehow for your extremism regarding Israel and the Jews?

A: I never suffered or even thought about my mother being Jewish. Only once in Ramallah a child yelled at me that my mother is Jewish. I don't have to prove myself. Not one of my friends is concerned with this fact.

Q: You know that according to Jewish religious law you are considered a Jew and are entitled to settle in Israel under the "law of return?"

A: First of all, I am Christian, although I am not at all religious. Secondly, this is neither a positive nor negative point. In any event, I do not regard the Jews as a people, but as a religion. There are Jews but no Jewish people.

Q: Can you define a "people." What are the criteria?

A: The Palestinians are a people. To be a people a group must have a culture, tradition, a common purpose, one language, and live in a territorial area.

Q: But that definition fits the Jews and Israel.

A: No. That's not so. Only a few of the world's Jews live in Israel.

Q: Today 2.5 million out of 12 million. But this is a continuing process. For generations Jews have lived outside of Israel and have looked forward to returning.

A: You said 12 million Jews but the Jews number 17 million. Hitler destroyed a half million Jews, not six million as you constantly claim.

Q: How were you caught?

A: They sold me out. Someone pointed me out in a café to an Israeli agent.

Q: Isn't it a fact that the Arab fighter is not loyal and is willing to betray his friends even without pressure? After all, you betrayed a comrade.

A: I don't accept this. It's true many informed on their friends but only because they were tortured. I'm certain of this. These are not things I have heard but I have actually seen them with my own eyes.

Q: What do the fedayeen mean by a "just solution" to the Mideast conflict?

A: Setting up a Palestinian state in which minorities would have equal rights, including Jews who consider themselves Arabs.

Q: How can a Jew be an Arab?

A: My mother for example. She's a Jewish Arab. And there are other Jews who are Arabs.

Q: Apparently you see a solution through the destruction of Israel by a war that will last generations.

A: I'm not worried. This is perhaps a matter for my son or grandson. We shall not stop until we seize power in this land. We'll drag the whole Arab world behind us. The Palestinians have always been an explosive element. We stand out in every political movement and trend.

Q: Nasser of Egypt has just accepted the United States peace initiative and has agreed in principle to enter peace talks with Israel.

A: That makes no difference. We'll go against Nasser. Just as we set him up we can depose him.

Q: It seems that the Palestinians have learned much from the Jews. Do you admit as much? Are you copying the Israelis?

A: You're right, we have learned from you. You have

been good teachers, but we shall attempt to surpass you.

Nasser then turned the interview around and asked a question: "Who in your opinion won the Six-Day War?"

"Israel, of course. She is now on the banks of the Suez, on the Jordan, and in the Syrian heights. The Russians have also won. They didn't fight but they gained from the war."

Nasser dismissed the visitor's answer. "I'm not joking," he said, "the real winners were the Palestinians. We have suddenly become a force to be reckoned with. Many acknowledge us. We are more organized now than ever before. As for your victory, you vanquished the Arab governments, not the Palestinians. It's not the same thing."

Q: Is there any possibility for a peaceful solution to the Arab-Israeli impasse?

A: There is no solution, only war. The only solution is that the full privileges and rights to this land will be in the hands of the Palestinians and not the Israelis. This will come only in war because we are stubborn and you are no less stubborn.

CHAPTER 12

The Enemy Within

The majority of the 333,000 Moslem and Christian Arabs living within Israel's pre-1967 borders have never accepted the existence of the Jewish state. This was the case before the Six-Day War and the feeling continues to this day. Only the Druzes, an Arab sect that has suffered persecution in the Mideast because of religious beliefs considered heretical by orthodox Moslems, and the Circassian minority are truly at peace with the State of Israel. The Druzes even serve in their own units in the Israeli army.

Indigenous resistance to Israel is chiefly expressed by the large Arab membership in the Arab faction of Israel's divided Communist party, the only non-Zionist party in the country's political life. Through their three elected members in the Knesset, Israel's parliament, the Arabs who vote Communist can voice the most extreme anti-Israel views.

Israel's Arab minority has never constituted a serious threat to the nation's security. Although over the years there have been several instances of espionage involving Israeli Arabs, the most serious cases of spying were uncovered among the Jewish population. Arabs arrested for espionage were usually found to be engaged in a fairly low level of intelligence-gathering on behalf of neighboring Arab countries.

Despite their feeling of enmity, Israel's Arabs until the Six-Day War did not play an active role in sabotage and terrorism against the Jewish population. Even during the period of the Egyptian fedayeen of the 1950s Israeli Arabs refrained from collaborating with the invading terrorists.

The depression and demoralization that swept the Arab world after the June, 1967, war also affected the Arab minority in Israel and gave rise to varying reactions. The wave of nationalistic spirit animating the Palestinian exiles in the refugee camps and cities of the Middle East did not excite the Arabs living in Israel for they had achieved a level of prosperity unknown in most Arab countries. At first renewed contacts between the Arabs of the newly occupied territories and their relatives from Israel found the latter boasting of their material gains. But soon Palestinian nationalists began influencing Israeli Arab youth, who for the first time experienced direct exposure to the bitterness and frustration of their displaced cousins.

The Israeli Arabs were told that their economic accomplishments did not count because they were not an independent people and would in time come to resemble the Israeli majority. Their national pride injured, many of Israel's Arabs grew increasingly receptive to the message of the Palestinian liberation movement and its tales of wondrous deeds against the Zionist enemy. A new atmosphere and new circumstances gave rise to hopes that the fedayeen would lead a Palestinian uprising.

Arabs from Israel and Arabs in the occupied areas could intermingle freely and it was easy for agents of the fedayeen to move about recruiting and indoctrinating new members of the Palestinian struggle. The Arabs of Israel, once labeled traitors by the extremists of the Arab world, were now invited into the ranks of the guerrillas. The spark of nationalism spurred many Israeli Arab youth to prove they were not collaborators with the Jews by supporting and aiding Fatah and the other groups.

The drastic geographical and political changes that took place after the Six-Day War enabled fifth columnists inside Israel to carry on more freely and complicated the task of Israel's security agencies. Before June, 1967, the *Shin Bet*, Israel's equivalent of the FBI, was mainly concerned with approximately 300,000 Arabs. Suddenly, an additional million Arabs had come under Israel's jurisdiction and the Shin Bet had no choice but to concentrate on the Arabs in the newly occupied zones because of their implacable hatred of Israel and the potential for unrest and sabotage.

As Israeli security agents and the police special branch concentrated on preventing fedayeen cells and bases from taking root on the West Bank and in the Gaza Strip, the surveillance of the Arab Palestinians living within the pre-1967 frontiers slackened. As a result, the fedayeen experienced some success in spreading their doctrine in the Arab towns and villages of northern Israel and the area in central Israel known as the "Little Triangle."

The number of Israeli Arabs arrested for sabotage rose sharply. Many Jews were shocked when a young Israeli Arab was arrested on charges of planting a time bomb in a Tel Aviv cinema. Subsequently, Arab students at the Hebrew University in Jerusalem played an important part in the bombing of the university's cafeteria. What surprised some Israelis was that the Arab youths involved in the cafeteria incident were from prosperous, prominent families on excellent terms with the Israeli authorities. Even Arab students who had declined to join fedayeen organizations participated in the terrorist action against their fellow students to the extent that they did not warn the Israeli authorities of the impending disaster.

In the three years following the Six-Day War, 140 Israeli Arabs were arrested for collaborating with terrorist groups. When seen against a total Arab population of 333,000 the number may seem small, but in comparison to the past, the readiness of several dozen Israeli Arab youths to take part in the murder of Israeli civilians showed that a significant development had taken place.

These Arabs, who had been subjected to intense propaganda and personal pressures, were in a position to do considerable damage because they knew Israel well and could point out her vulnerable points. Their fluent Hebrew and social contacts with the Jewish population—some of them had Jewish girl friends—meant they could help plan attacks on vital installations. One Israeli Arab working on behalf of the fedayeen was worth more to the terrorists than ten Arabs from the occupied territories or the neighboring Arab countries. It was thus that the most serious acts of sabotage carried out inside Israel's original borders were the work of Israeli Arabs.

Some Israeli Arab youth were so anxious to join fedayeen groups that they often took the initiative without waiting for fedayeen recruiters to arrive in their village. More often than not these young men would find their way to Fatah or another unit as individuals, but on some occasions groups of youths from one area or village would organize themselves and make contact with a fedayeen group. This happened in the Galilee village of Touran where twenty young men joined together and sent envoys to Lebanon to contact Fatah. The couriers arrived in Lebanon, were trained by the fedayeen and set out to return to their village. They encountered an Israeli army patrol and were killed in an exchange of fire.

Interrogation of Israeli Arabs arrested for terrorism revealed they were mostly Moslem villagers from comfortable circumstances. Many had Israeli friends and some even had Jewish mistresses. Usually the families of the arrested saboteurs were ignorant of their activities.

Israel's policy of punishment inside her borders was different from the measures adopted in the occupied areas. Israeli Arabs arrested for terrorism were treated more leniently than their counterparts on the West Bank and Gaza. An Arab in the occupied zones charged with terrorism runs the danger of having his home blown up, whereas members of Israel's minorities charged with the same crimes are not subjected to this even though they represent a definite danger to Israel's security. Minister of Defense Moshe Dayan has rejected suggestions that Israeli Arabs be treated the same and that their houses also be dynamited. Dayan feels it is important to preserve as fully as possible the civil liberties and open society enjoyed by Israel's Arabs.

When incidents of sabotage increased toward the end of 1969, proposals were made that the military administration of the Arab areas be reinstituted—it had been abolished some years earlier. The Shin Bet decided the system of controlling the internal movements of all Arabs by means of special passes would be ineffective. Instead, administrative measures were introduced, including prohibiting some 700 Israeli Arabs from traveling to the occupied territories and approximately 100 persons from traveling freely within Israel.

A more serious problem for Israel existed in the occupied territories where the fedayeen hoped to realize widespread support for their guerrilla war. Directly after the Six-Day War, leaders of Fatah transferred their military headquarters to the West Bank. Arafat was optimistic that the populace of the Arab lands under Israeli control would progress rapidly from a guerrilla struggle to a large-scale popular uprising. But more than four years after the June war the fedayeen were bitterly disappointed by their failure to achieve their goal of waging war against Israel inside her territory.

Within a few months of June, 1967, it was evident that the majority of Arabs in the captured areas were not prepared to take up arms against the Israeli occupation. There was, to be sure, considerable sympathy for the extremist aims of the Palestinian militants as well as a readiness to cooperate in some ways. There was not, however, any prospect for a coordinated, mass confrontation with Israeli forces. For this to come about the Arabs would have to achieve a unity and solidarity they have never exhibited. Before the Six-Day War, Fatah and other fedayeen groups had worked toward a popular war of liberation, but when the time came the behavior of the Arab civilian population was marked by apathy and refusal to join regular Arab armies in attempting to repel advancing Israeli troops.

Fedayeen leaders had been frustrated many times in their calls for uprisings by the Arab masses in Israel, and later, the occupied territories. Fedayeen ideology often cites the power of the Arab masses to wage a genuine people's struggle against the "Zionist oppressor." The reality of the Arab experience after the Six-Day War showed the fedayeen how illusory their appraisal of the capacities of their Palestinian brethren was.

The leadership of the Palestinians in the occupied territories was thrown for a loss as a result of the Six-Day War. In Gaza there had never developed a leadership strong enough to influence the Arabs crowded into a tiny strip of land. For years Egypt had undermined and weakened any leaders in Gaza.

In Judea and Samaria the situation was different. Since annexation of the West Bank in 1949 by Jordan's King Abdullah and during the years of rule by Hussein, Abdullah's grandson, political figures and intelligentsia emerged to form a Palestinian opposition to Hashemite rule. But the trauma of June, 1967, caused a setback to the political leaders and they were relegated to a secondary, behind-the-scenes role. Day-to-day contacts between the local population and the Israeli military government became the responsibility of the municipal leaders. Mayors and village mukthars became the key figures on the West Bank. By means of a "give-and-take" approach toward them, the Israeli military governor was able to keep track of any incipient rebellions or disruptive movements. As the people responsible for the continued supply of vital services—electricity, water, etc.—the municipal leaders were afraid of any movements that might interfere with the smooth functioning of commercial and civic life on the West Bank. Consequently, these officials were vulnerable to pressure, both from the Israeli authorities and the Arab merchants who wanted a return to normalcy.

On the West Bank the pragmatic nature of the leadership prevented the population from taking up the fedayeen cause en masse. The Arab leaders interested in peaceful existence under the Israeli occupation felt their way was correct not because of any desire to aid Israel but because they had seen that the Arab armies and governments had been unable to defeat Israel and had dragged the Palestinians down with them. Town and village seniors of the West Bank also felt they had to preserve civil order in their area or run the danger of pushing Israeli occupation forces into evacuating the indigenous Arabs and annexing the land. This view was expressed by Sheikh Muhammed Ali Jabari, Mayor of Hebron and a determined opponent of collaboration with the fedayeen, when he said: "Terrorism endangers the lives and livelihoods of the residents of Hebron and pushes them toward emigration from their lands. All this is not in the interests of the Arabs."

The Arab population was buffeted by conflicting emotions and experiences. Hardly had they absorbed the impact of the Arab defeat in the June war than they were confronted with thousands of Israeli visitors. They were deeply curious about a people with whom they had had no contact for nineteen years and many reunions took place between Jewish families and Arab friends from the pre-1948 period. Many business relations developed from these first contacts, but eventually fedayeen terrorism put an end to the Israeli visits. The fedayeen strongly disapproved of these friendly contacts with the "Zionists" and attacked Israeli civilians. There was a spate of incidents including ambushes of Israeli vehicles and the murdering of civilians in marketplaces. In some instances non-Jewish American tourists were killed and injured when grenades were thrown at their touring buses.

Fedayeen violence accomplished its aim: tourist traffic to the West Bank decreased sharply. Only persons who had to travel there risked entering the dangerous zone. Contact between Jew and Arab ended as each side closed itself off in a cocoon of suspicion.

Israelis have always known that the sympathy of the Arabs living in the occupied territories is with the fedayeen. No matter how well-regarded Israel's accomplishments are and how eagerly her aid is accepted the Palestinians of Gaza and the West Bank are not happy living under an Israeli occupation. Antipathy toward the occupier notwithstanding, most of the Arabs were not ready to act violently against Israel.

The Israeli authorities have maintained as liberal and humane an administration as possible to avoid a situation wherein cruel repression would drive the Arabs to acts of armed resistance. Freedom of expression is permitted and collective punishment usually avoided. Israel's occupation policy is intended to prevent as much as possible clashes with the nationalistic and religious feelings of the people in the territories while aiding the area's development.

Travel to the East Bank by Arabs was permitted without restriction, including pilgrimages to Mecca. Young Arabs were allowed to study at schools in the Arab countries. The military government was also careful to stay clear of internal political affairs and in this connection even Arab advocates of integrating the occupied areas into Israel received no encouragement.

Freedom of expression was a mainstay of Israel's occupation policy despite the fedayeen threat. More freedom exists now than prior to the Six-Day War when Hussein controlled the West Bank and Egypt administered the Gaza Strip. Sermons by Moslem religious leaders are transmitted directly from Al Aksa mosque in Jerusalem by the Israel Broadcasting Authority; foreign correspondents are allowed to interview Arabs living under occupation and *Al Kuds*, an Arabic newspaper published in Jerusalem, is not censored politically. These and other tangible proofs that the occupation has not suppressed liberty of thought, no matter how anti-Israel, exist in abundance. In the schools anti-Semitic sentiments and defamatory references to Israel have been deleted from texts but no attempt has been made to replace these Arabic books with texts printed in Israel. Diplomas given secondary school graduates are the same as before June, 1967, to enable the students to gain admission to college in Arab countries.

One concern of the occupation has been to limit the visibility of Israeli military and official personnel. Soldiers are not stationed inside the cities and the number of civilian employes working in Israel's occupation apparatus is kept at a minimum—on the West Bank there are only 357 Israeli civilian employes, while the Arab bureaucracy in the same region numbers 7500 employes. In Gaza the educational system comprises 1750 employes of which only five are Israeli.

The "open bridge" policy whereby free movement of thousands of West Bank Arabs and goods to the East Bank and beyond are allowed is also a function of Israel's occupation policy. Although maintaining this policy has meant security problems, Defense Minister Dayan feels it is an essential aspect of the post-1967 situation, one that will be of considerable significance in helping to normalize Arab-Israeli relations when and if a peace settlement is reached. Through the commercial exchanges carried on between the West Bank Arabs and Arabs on the other side many Israeli products, ranging from oranges to medicine, have found their way to the Arab world. Arab workers have found employment in Israel and the West Bank's economic development has been enhanced under Israeli occupation.

The fedayeen and the neighboring Arab countries called on the Arabs under Israeli occupation to totally boycott the Israeli administration, but these appeals have failed because the Arabs need the Israelis and cooperate of their own accord. Jordan has tried to encourage general strikes on the West Bank. Hussein thought that by continuing to pay the salaries of civil servants he would exercise some control over them. Millions of Jordanian dinars sent from Amman to the West Bank were meant to keep Arab municipal workers from showing up at their jobs. The Jordanian move did not achieve the desired results and only the judges and lawyers of the West Bank kept up their strike because they could not hope to earn as much practicing as they were being paid by Hussein. Jordan even continued paying salaries after the former Hashemite employes were on the payrolls of the Israeli military administration. It turned out that the community workers of the West Bank enjoyed an unprecedented situation: double salaries.

Most opposition to Israeli rule was passive but the fedayeen tried to expand general strikes into acts of civil disobedience. There was no shortage of appropriate dates for Arab strikes—November 2, the anniversary of the Balfour declaration; November 29, the date the United Nations voted in 1947 to partition Palestine into Jewish and Arab states; Israel Independence Day, May 15; and the anniversary of the outbreak of the Six-Day War were just some of the occasions for calling strikes. Instructions were broadcast over the Arab radio stations and were also passed on from fedayeen headquarters by travelers passing over to the West Bank from Jordan.

Demonstrators were allowed to express themselves without restraint and this accounts for many placards calling for the extermination of the Jews. Marching protestors would often chant, "*Itbah al Yahud*" (Slaughter the Jews) and following the Baghdad hangings in which nine Jews were executed publicly, Arab demonstrators carried a sign reading: "*Shukran ya Bagdad*" (Thank you Baghdad).

Israeli soldiers did not intervene in demonstrations as long as they kept to assigned streets. When student manifestations worsened and exploded into rock-throwing melees several schools were closed by the military governor and were only reopened after parents and teachers pledged to prevent any further reckless demonstrations. Despite the often unruly appearance of the protests and frequent clashes between demonstrators and Israeli troops not one Arab was killed on the West Bank. In Gaza, an Arab woman was killed in one incident and the Israeli officer responsible was court-martialed. The occupation authorities were scrupulous in maintaining discipline among Israeli military personnel stationed in occupied zones. In February, 1971, Moshe Dayan reported to the Knesset, Israel's parliament, that thirty residents of the Gaza Strip were injured by "unwarranted and unauthorized violence" at the hands of Israeli troops sent in to curb a rash of fedayeen attacks a month earlier. As a result, Dayan said, one Israeli officer and a number of enlisted men were to be brought before a disciplinary court. Dayan also reported that three officers had received administrative reprimands and three soldiers were sentenced to thirty-five days in jail for stealing from Arab residents in Gaza.

After a few waves of unruly demonstrations and civil disorders on the West Bank things quieted down toward the end of 1969 as the Arabs realized they themselves and not Israel were the chief victims of the demonstrations, strikes, and fedayeen vengeance killings. The fedayeen failed to become a political factor in the occupied territories. They were disappointed by the local population's lack of receptivity to their appeal for a popular uprising. The fedayeen were aware of the sympathy of the Arabs but also realized there was little chance they would risk their way of life in another war with Israel. This realization drove the Palestinian extremists to try to disrupt the normalization that had set in. They aimed at thwarting the rising standard of living and joint Arab-Israeli undertakings in the territories. Even the showing of a film under Israeli auspices was obnoxious to the fedayeen and they did not hesitate to terrorize their fellow Arabs attending cinemas in Gaza and other towns by throwing grenades into the theaters.

Most of the Arabs on the West Bank were unlikely prospects for recruitment by the fedayeen but some youths were attracted to the Palestine liberation movement and crossed to the East Bank where they were trained by several guerrilla and terrorist groups. This method seemed less dangerous to them than joining the fedayeen who had arrived on the West Bank to carry out sabotage. In most cases assistance to the fedayeen was extended by the West Bank and Gaza Arabs in less direct ways—hiding them out and giving them food and advice on local conditions. But many Arab residents were not willing to even assist the terrorists indirectly for fear of being caught and punished.

In Gaza the fedayeen were more successful. Israeli authorities found that as many as eighty percent of those youths approached by the fedayeen responded affirmatively. Those that refused to join were often coerced or condemned to death by kangaroo courts. The population of the Gaza Strip is poorer than that of the West Bank and over 200,000 of its close to 400,000 residents are impoverished refugees living in giant U.N.-supported camps. It is natural that in their squalor and despair these Palestinians should become enthusiastic supporters of the fedayeen. The successful appeal of the fedayeen in Gaza is demonstrated by the high rate of terrorist attacks carried out there. The absence of influential leading families also made it difficult for the Israeli authorities to deal with the population there.

The overwhelming majority of those killed and injured in the frequent fedayeen grenade attacks in Gaza were Arabs. Over 1000 innocent Arabs, including women and children have been hurt in these incidents, many of them maimed for life. Between June, 1967, and June, 1971, 219 Arabs were killed by fedayeen.

Because of overcrowding, the congested layout of houses and other circumstances, such as the large number of dilapidated structures, refugee camps offered especially convenient conditions for terror operations. In the summer of 1971, Israeli authorities took measures to ensure safety and security in the camps. This included the construction of access roads within the camps, involving in certain places the demolition of some dwellings. No demolition took place unless alternative housing, of at least equal standard, was provided for the occupants of the house. In most instances, the new accommodations are of a higher standard. If the occupants preferred new housing of their own choice to accommodations offered by the authorities they were free to avail themselves of such housing. The evacuees received financial grants to defray the cost of moving into the new accommodations. Arrangements were made to enable the evacuees to continue in their old employment. Whenever necessary, new employment was provided.

During the nineteen years of Egyptian occupation the Gaza Strip was virtually a concentration camp; its population subjected to endless restrictions, deprived of freedom of movement, barred from sources of livelihood, terrorized by a military regime of repression. The jails were filled with political suspects and torture was commonplace.

On the West Bank, as well as in Gaza, many of the fedayeen victims were Arabs who traveled daily to work in Israel. Dozens of Arab workers were killed and injured by grenades thrown by fedayeen into their buses. At one point in Gaza—in the beginning of 1970—ninety percent of fedayeen terrorism was directed against Arab men and women employed in Israeli enterprises and merchants who conducted business with Israeli companies. Thousands of Palestinian refugees who had found employment in Israel after years of enforced idleness left Gaza and moved to the West Bank where they felt safer and where the leaders had prevailed on the fedayeen from time to time to refrain from harming Arab workers. Often workers subject to attack were related to fedayeen.

Palestinian extremists also attacked Arabs of the occupied areas who dared to disagree with the doctrines of Fatah or the PFLP. On the West Bank, Fatah threatened the lives and attacked the homes of Aziz Shahada and Dr. M. Farouki, prominent figures who publicly expressed their support for the concept of a Palestinian state on the West Bank. Many Arabs suspected of having connections with Israeli security agencies were murdered, and in the fall of 1969 fedayeen pretending to be Israeli soldiers killed six notables in the town of Halhul near Hebron. When the assassins were captured by Israel a few months later they said they had received their instruction in code in a broadcast over the Fatah radio station in Cairo, *Kol Haatsifa.*

Israel's occupation policy has been based on the avoidance of excessive or cruel punishments, the holding of hostages, or collective retribution involving the guilty as well as the innocent. There have been exceptions to this policy, but on the whole it has remained in effect. When curfews are imposed for the purpose of searching for terrorists or an economic blockade is directed against a certain area, it is true that the entire population suffers a certain deprivation. On the other hand, these collective measures have been effective in persuading municipal leaders to press for a cessation of fedayeen violence.

There were two cases of drastic departures from Israel's established punishment policy and each time a sharp debate and widespread controversy within Israel resulted. The first occasion followed the murder of a Jewish merchant in Gaza in October, 1969. The victim had been in partnership with an Arab and had done much to facilitate the marketing in Israel proper of furniture made in Gaza. The Israeli military government was angered over the failure of neighboring shopkeepers to warn the victim when they learned the day before of the fedayeen plot. After lengthy discussion, Moshe Dayan authorized the blowing up of buildings located near the corner where the killing had occurred. Four of the buildings were residences and the remainder were used as warehouses.

The other instance of collective punishment also took place in the fall of 1969 following the killing of an Israeli officer in a fedayeen ambush near Halhul, where earlier six Arabs had been murdered. Dayan came to Halhul to offer his condolences to the village elders and while there even offered them weapons to defend themselves against terrorists. The elders assured the Defense Minister that none of the villagers had aided the fedayeen. Shortly after the death of the Israeli officer several fedayeen were arrested in Halhul and it was decided to demolish twenty-four houses in the part of the village where the fedayeen had hidden out. The assumption on Israel's part was that the residents of this sector knew about the presence of the Palestinian terrorists and gave them aid. About half of the houses dynamited were uninhabited.

Punishment by destroying property rather than taking lives was considered the lesser evil by the Israeli military government. It was of the opinion that destroying Arab property is a more potent deterrent than either personal imprisonment or levying fines.

Another effective Israeli countermeasure was the exiling of dissident leaders to the East Bank of the Jordan. By December, 1969, several dozen Arab political figures had been banished to the East Bank after being charged by Israel with incitement, organizing strikes and maintaining contacts with terrorist organizations. In this way Israel avoided arresting notables and imposed further difficulties on fedayeen seeking to organize the Arabs. Within a short time the exiled personalities lost their special status in the eyes of the Jordanian authorities and the fedayeen leaders and were regarded as refugees cut off from homes and family. Their fate made an impression on agitators remaining in the occupied areas and served as a further deterrent against disorders and rebellion.

Jordan saw that the trend of exiling troublemakers was thinning the ranks of the West Bank leaders and threatening to eliminate a Palestinian leadership altogether. Consequently, Amman announced at the end of

1969 that Jordan would no longer admit West Bank Arabs exiled by Israel.

The Israeli authorities employed house demolition and personal banishment on a relatively wide scale in their struggle against the fedayeen, but they avoided executing terrorist offenders. Despite a provision for the death sentence in the emergency measures the military governor was ordered not to ask the courts for the death sentence in cases of terrorism. The policy has been criticized by Israeli security officials who argue that a distinction should be made between fedayeen who try to penetrate Israel as guerrillas, usually dressed in some type of uniform, and fedayeen who act as terrorists, striking at civilians and killing innocent women and children. The latter, the critics say, should be given the death sentence while the former should be treated like military prisoners of war. Prominent among those opposing the overall policy of no capital punishment is Israel's former premier, David Ben Gurion, who maintains that the abolition of capital punishment in Israel (the final Knesset decision was taken on February 16, 1954) did not pertain to acts of treason during time of war or for crimes of genocide. In Ben Gurion's view, the fedayeen seek to destroy the Jewish people in Israel. The Nazis, Ben Gurion points out, intended the annihilation of the Jews throughout the world, while the Arabs desire the liquidation of the Jews of Palestine. This is genocide, the former Israeli head of state argues in stressing the validity of the death sentence as just punishment for Palestinian terrorists. He asserts, however, that the Arab soldier should be accorded the respect deserved by a military adversary who is not to blame for following orders that originate with "genocidal" Arab leaders.

CHAPTER 13

Russia and China

*Among the large amounts of Arab weapons cap*tured by Israeli forces in the Gaza Strip during the Six-Day War were several thousand Kalashnikov automatic rifles manufactured by Communist China under license from the Soviet Union. In arsenals belonging to the Palestine Liberation Organization, Chinese-made equipment was found in large quantities. The mines, explosives, hand grenades, machine guns, rockets, and small arms were new and markings on several crates indicated that the shipments entered the Middle East through an Iraqi port. These armaments were proof of the close relations existing between the Palestinian liberation movement and Communist China.

In March, 1965, a few months after the creation of the Palestine Liberation Organization by the Arab Summit Conference, the head of the P.L.O., Ahmed Shukairy, was invited to Peking. China's leaders realized that the Mideast conflict was an opportunity for agitating against both the United States and the Soviet Union. The instrument of Chinese activity would be the emerging fedayeen movement. Thus began the flirtation between the Palestinians and Peking, a relationship that was to survive Shukairy and continue to the present time.

Despite the fact that diplomatic ties between China and Egypt were frequently strained, Shukairy risked Nasser's displeasure by publicizing his new friendship with the giant Asian power. Soon after his visit to Peking he invited the Chinese Ambassador in Cairo to accompany him to Gaza where he delivered a particularly vitriolic speech against Israel to a Palestinian audience. Shukairy also began affecting the style of China's leaders and in several public appearances sported a Mao-type tunic.

In August, 1966, when the P.L.O. was competing with the ascendant Fatah, Shukairy proudly announced that a group of P.L.O. youths had just returned from China where they had undergone special military training. This was the beginning of guerrilla training generously extended by China to several leftist fedayeen groups over the years, including Fatah, the Popular Front for the Liberation of Palestine and the Popular Democratic Front for the Liberation of Palestine.

The number of fedayeen traveling to China for training increased sharply after the Six-Day War. Courses were expanded to include training for fedayeen commanders as well as lower-ranking members. In addition to a thorough grounding in Mao Tse-tung's political and guerrilla warfare doctrines, the Palestinians toured China and were introduced to high-level leaders. On their return from China many fedayeen stopped over in North Vietnam and North Korea to further cement ties between the Palestinian movement and Asian Communism.

Communist China's interest in the Middle East as a testing ground for its theories of international revolution and a potential hot point in East-West confrontations was revealed well before the formation of the P.L.O. In December, 1963, Premier Chou En-lai toured Asia and Africa. On his arrival in Cairo he issued a statement denouncing American and Russian penetration of the Middle East and promising China's respect for the sovereignty of the Arab nations.

China also mobilized considerable propaganda in support of the P.L.O. In 1966, the Afro-Asian Writers' Emergency Meeting in Peking concluded by issuing a resolution, which among other things equated Zionism with colonialism, condemned Israel for providing strategic aid to "certain puppet governments" in Africa, and pledged the efforts of all revolutionary writers and "progressive" parties and organizations to oppose "Zionist infiltration" in their own countries. The resolution, as reported in the *Peking Review* of July 15, 1966, announces the meeting's support for "the struggle waged by the Palestine Liberation Organization to liberate Palestine."

In February, 1966, the Vietcong sent a message to the P.L.O. protesting against the sale of U.S. tanks to Israel and pledging support of the South Vietnamese people for the "just and patriotic" Palestinian struggle for "freedom and independence." The message, released by Hanoi Radio's international service in English, said, "May the friendship and militant solidarity between the South Vietnamese and Palestine people develop splendidly with every day."

In May, 1967, China was the first country to issue statements supporting the Arabs and calling for Israel's destruction. Following the Six-Day War, China lost no time in characterizing Israel as America's "police dog" in the Middle East. "Without orders from the U.S. Israel would lack both the courage and means to carry out such armed aggression," the Chinese propaganda asserted. Some observers found a bit of irony in the fact that Israel had been the first Mideastern nation to recognize Communist China in early 1950. Peking, however, never established diplomatic relations with Israel.

Communist China tried hard to extend her influence in the Middle East. Despite Peking's Marxist rejection of organized religion, a Chinese Islamic Association was formed and its leaders took part in the pilgrimage to Mecca as part of a well-publicized excursion that combined political aims with religious fervor. Leftist subversive elements in Arab countries were given money and an effort was made to alter the pro-Moscow orientation of the Arab Communist parties. China's policy brought her into conflict with the established Arab regimes, and a serious falling out with Egypt occurred after Peking revealed its support for the anti-Nasserist regime in Iraq.

China realized that her chances of supplanting the Soviet Union's influence in Egypt were slim, especially since Moscow was giving Nasser massive aid and extending full diplomatic support for Egypt in international bodies where China was not represented. Instead of courting Egypt, China decided to go all the way with the Palestinians as her protégés. Even though the P.L.O. was sponsored by Egypt, China accorded the Shukairy group full diplomatic status in Peking.

The Arab defeat in the Six-Day War provided another opportunity for China to exacerbate tensions in the

Mideast—principally against Russia—and to increase her support of the fedayeen. Peking informed the Arabs that one of the principal reasons for their defeat was Russia's betrayal and Moscow's neo-colonialist policy. Peking claimed that Moscow refused to extend help to the Arabs during the Six-Day War and afterwards, together with the United States, imposed a cease-fire on the Arab states. When addressing themselves to the Palestinians the Chinese stressed a popular war of liberation, similar to that being waged in Vietnam, as the only means of eventually defeating Israel.

In an article discussing the lessons to be derived from the 1967 war against "Israeli aggression," the *Peking Review* of September, 1967, advised the Arabs to devote their attention to a war of attrition against Israel in an effort to drive her from the occupied territories.

Peking found a common language with the fedayeen. At the same time relations cooled with the Arab governments because the latter were reluctant to antagonize Russia by maintaining excessively close ties with the Chinese. China was the only country outside the Middle East to totally reject a compromise Middle East settlement. When Egypt, Jordan, and Israel accepted Secretary of State Rogers's peace initiative in the summer of 1970 and agreed to enter the Jarring talks, China officially praised the fedayeen who rejected the United States bid. "The proposal for a political settlement in the Middle East is a criminal attempt to allow one or two great powers to once again divide the region into spheres of influence and put an end to the Palestinian cause," a Peking statement asserted. When Palestinian terrorists hijacked international jet liners and held civilians hostage in September, 1970, China expressed her approval of the action. PFLP leader George Habash spent a lot of time in China, North Korea, and North Vietnam at the time of the hijackings. He is believed to have received substantial moral and financial support from the Asian Communists for his group's daring undertaking.

In addition to arms, China took pains to keep the fedayeen well supplied with propaganda. Arabic versions of works by Mao were sent in large quantities to the guerrilla organizations. Every time an Israeli army unit attacked a fedayeen base, pamphlets and other materials printed in China were found in abundance. But in all probability it was superior weaponry rather than the thoughts of Chairman Mao that most impressed the fedayeen. China responded affirmatively to each Palestinian request for more advanced equipment. When the fedayeen had difficulty hitting Israeli settlements across the border they received long-range Katyusha rockets made in China. By launching them from Lebanese territory they were able to inflict heavy damage on Jewish civilian targets.

Since her entry in the United Nations, mainland China has championed the fedayeen in debates on the Middle East and informed diplomatic observers are convinced that China will block any peace agreement that could be seen as selling out the Palestinians.

The Soviet Union became seriously concerned over the inroads made by China among the fedayeen. Russia had not been able to gain a foothold with the Palestinian extremists, partly because she consistently displayed an ambivalent attitude toward them. The Kremlin wanted to exercise some control over the Palestinian movement, which was steadily gaining strength and eliciting a sympathetic response in the Arab world. Russia realized that neglecting the fedayeen would only aid China's efforts. But the Soviet Union also feared the reckless extremism of the guerrillas and knew it would be difficult to exert pressure on them. Moscow was apprehensive over the fedayeen potential for bringing about a confrontation with the United States. While the Russians were willing to give full aid to the Arab states and those elements under their control they were afraid of directly assisting the Palestinian groups.

A partial solution to Moscow's dilemma was to render the fedayeen moral support. Soviet newspapers praised the heroics of Fatah and other organizations in bombastic pronouncements but declined to endorse the Palestinian aim of destroying Israel. The fedayeen used Russian weapons, but at first these weapons were received via the Egyptian and Syrian armies rather than directly from the Soviet Union.

Russia's ambiguity toward the fedayeen was also expressed in her reactions to Palestinian terrorism. When the PFLP began its campaign of planting explosives in centers of civilian population, Moscow denounced the actions. Radio Moscow expressed approval of "legitimate guerrilla operations that are necessary acts of resistance against the illegitimate conqueror." The extremist perpetrators of such non-guerrilla deeds as the blowing up of a supermarket in Jerusalem and a cafeteria at the Hebrew University were denounced by Radio Moscow as "inhuman crimes."

Russia surprisingly also refused to back the fedayeen at the International Red Cross Conference in Istanbul in 1969 where they requested international legal status. Recognition at this time would have had far-reaching implications and would have bestowed upon the Palestinian terrorists the status of freedom fighters.

For a long time Russia preferred to keep her contacts with the fedayeen secret. In January, 1970, shortly before

Yasir Arafat left for his first official visit to the Soviet Union, it was suddenly revealed that for the past two years the leader of Al Fatah had been secretly visiting Moscow. In September, 1968, when Nasser visited the Soviet Union, Arafat also journeyed there with a deputy. The Kremlin was not able to continue to refuse fedayeen demands that Arafat finally be invited openly to visit Russia.

In February, 1970, a seven-man delegation consisting of Arafat, members of Saiqah, the Popular Democratic Front for the Liberation of Palestine and the Arab Liberation Forces left for Moscow. It was the first official fedayeen mission to visit the Soviet capital. The invitation had been extended by the Soviet Committee for Afro-Asian solidarity. In this way Russia was able to avoid according the fedayeen the prestige of a state visit. Nevertheless, the fedayeen met the Soviet leadership in the Kremlin. These meetings were not mentioned in the Russian press, which continued hammering away at the official Soviet Mideast line: insistence on total Israeli withdrawal from the occupied territories and the endorsement of peace negotiations under Big Four auspices.

Despite the reservations, it was evident that a new period of Soviet-fedayeen relations began in 1970. Russia's apprehension over losing any influence whatever with the terrorist groups and the possibility of exploiting the fedayeen in Moscow's campaign against pro-Western Arab regimes were basic reasons for the new attitudes. The ascendancy of the fedayeen in the Arab world had suggested many new opportunities to the men in the Kremlin. Soviet agents encouraged fedayeen to seek the overthrow of Hussein in Jordan, an action that hastened the guerrillas' expulsion from that country.

Newly strengthened ties included a direct method of

distributing Soviet arms to the fedayeen thereby doing away with the Egyptians and Syrians as middlemen. The conciliatory moves Russia has made toward the fedayeen were not occasioned by ideological motives. If it had not been for the success of Communist China in wooing the Palestinians it is likely the Soviet Union would still be treating Yasir Arafat and other Palestinian leaders with the contemptuous condescension powerful and confident adults reserve for obstreperous infants. The decline of the fedayeen in Jordan and Russia's heavy involvement in Egypt's political affairs, as well as her military establishment, necessitated a somewhat toned-down, more detached Kremlin policy toward the Palestinians. Nevertheless, the fedayeen, like so many other factors in the Middle East, may have another day, and the Soviet Union, which maintains an elaborate and highly skilled diplomatic and intelligence presence in the region, will be alert to any development that might suggest the desirability of increased support for the Palestinians.

CHAPTER 14

The Future of the Fedayeen

The seemingly final eclipse of the fedayeen in 1971 convinced many observers that the Palestinian guerrilla movement had had its day. An estimated 700 fedayeen out of 3000 were killed by King Hussein's troops in Jordan in the summer of 1971 and only 500 remained in Jordan. Many fled to Lebanon where over 3000 guerrillas were gathered in bases in the south at the beginning of 1972. A remaining 2000 were located in Syria, where the government kept them under tight control.

The future of the fedayeen was seriously in doubt and their prospects for threatening Israel or successfully continuing as the spearhead of Palestinian nationalism were unpromising, in the view of many students of Arab affairs. But perhaps this tendency to write them off failed to recognize that what so often seems to be final in the Middle East is in reality only ephemeral. The renewal of fedayeen attacks from Lebanese territory in the first weeks of 1972 and Israeli reprisal raids suggested that in certain circumstances the Palestine armed struggle could experience a revival.

In reviewing some of the fedayeen's failures and accomplishments since the Six-Day War, it seems that their most notable achievement was the reawakening of a spirit of nationalism and ethnic identity among a people who had been in a state of political and social stagnation since the end of the 1936–39 period of guerrilla war against the British and Jewish settlement in Palestine. The rise of the fedayeen contributed to international consciousness of the Palestinian problem.

The actions of the fedayeen can be credited with making many westerners realize that the basic conflict in the Middle East is between the Palestinians and Israel. The Arab-Israel dispute emanates from the Palestine problem and it is doubtful if any future Middle East settlement will be effective if it does not somehow satisfy the aspirations of the Palestinians.

Israeli thinking on the Palestinian issue is often divided along generational lines. Premier Golda Meir and other political leaders of her pioneer generation have been skeptical of the validity of a Palestinian identity and claim to nationhood. They tend to reject the notion of a separate accommodation with the Palestinians, claiming that since Jordan is de facto Palestinian there is no need to create another Palestinian state in the West Bank. Israelis can recall 1947 when an attempt to set up an Arab-Palestinian state was rejected and subsequent attempts to negotiate the conflict failed.

Nevertheless, the younger generation of Israeli leaders reveal somewhat different attitudes than the European-born old guard. Defense Minister Moshe Dayan has shown himself to be sensitive to the feelings of the Palestinians and has occasionally expressed his thoughts on the subject. He once reported to a student gathering in Tel Aviv on his meeting with Fadwa Touken, a young Palestinian poet from Nablus. He read the students a Hebrew translation of one of her moving and emphatically nationalistic poems about Jerusalem called, "My City, Occupied," and then to the surprised audience Moshe Dayan said, "We have to make an effort to establish contacts with the million Arabs with whom and next to whom we are destined to live. We have to understand their background, their emotional climate, whether we like it or not. I know only too well that at this stage, at first, this will be a one-way road; even if we understand them, they will not understand us. But even so, we have to go and listen to them in the hope that one day they will listen to us."

But Dayan is reluctant to encourage Palestinian political aspirations because he feels that their ultimate aim is the removal of Israel from the map. Deputy Premier Yigal Allon has broken with the view of much of the Israeli leadership by advocating the setting up of autonomous, self-governing bodies on the West Bank as a first step toward home rule. According to the Allon Plan, the first stage of eventual autonomous rule would give the Palestinian inhabitants of the West Bank responsibility for their own municipal, economic, educational, and cultural affairs. They would be permitted to establish economic and cultural ties with other Arab nations, even if Israel were still in a state of war with these countries. In the second stage of West Bank independence, the Palestinian leadership would assume responsibility for security and domestic order and the inhabitants of the area would be granted the right of self-determination. They could choose to remain as an independent Palestinian state or work out a form of merger or federation with Jordan. Allon's plan is one of several indications of the readiness of Israel's younger leaders to recognize Palestinian national rights and attempt to reach some agreement that would provide for a measure of Palestinian self-determination.

The fedayeen have consistently rejected any notion of accommodation with continued Jewish existence in the disputed land and have thwarted any conciliatory Israeli approach. They have contributed to the prolongation of muddled and ineffectual third-party efforts to settle the region's conflict. Offsetting fedayeen intransigence, however, have been new political expressions among Palestinians on the West Bank. The clash of Hussein and the fedayeen convinced some West Bank leaders that their best hope was to relinquish ideas of rejoining Jordan and to find some approach toward settlement with Israel. As a first step they agreed to participate in elections for municipal office held under Israeli auspices but conducted according to Jordanian law, i.e. voting rights for property-owning men only.

The suppression of the fedayeen by the Jordanian army and the prosperity of West Bank Arabs due to improved agriculture and their participation in Israeli economic life were the major factors behind a new readiness to regularize the political status of the West Bank and negotiate with the Israelis. The Palestinians of the West Bank, where the fedayeen presence has been erased, now openly discuss ideas of autonomy and permanent peace. Perhaps this new trend in political attitudes will succeed in bridging the chasm of fear, hatred, and prejudice that has separated Palestinian and Jew. But it would be overly optimistic to expect too much from these initial and hesitant moves.

The fedayeen, bereft of propaganda and political

successes, may face the loss of support they have found among the Palestinians. Perhaps a more realistic leadership will emerge once the current cycle of Arab radicalization ends. But until that happens the Palestinian cause, with the encouragement of Communist China and third-world nations, will be cast in terms of revolutionary war against Israel with the ultimate aim of eliminating the Jewish presence in the Middle East. As Yasir Arafat has often said: "The Palestinian people will never stop until it reaches the shores of Jaffa and Haifa."

Within the Arab world the fedayeen are embroiled in strife and discord. Whatever the Palestinian guerrillas may have done to improve Arab morale, the Arabs have paid for dearly. Fatah was a precipitating factor in bringing on the Six-Day War and following that disaster, the fedayeen were instrumental in causing several crises and threatening the sovereignty of Jordan and Lebanon. In Jordan, Hussein's actions against the fedayeen were crueler than anything they experienced in their conflict with Israel. It took Hussein more than two years before he moved decisively against the guerrillas but when he did his offensive was determined and relentless.

Hussein had never been happy with the rise of the fedayeen movement within his borders. He feared Israeli reprisals and was uneasy over the dissident Palestinian population in his country. In the initial phase of fedayeen action after the Six-Day War, Hussein's opposition to Fatah and the Popular Front for the Liberation of Palestine was rejected by members of the King's cabinet and many officers in his army. Following Israel's major strike at Karameh in March, 1968, fedayeen propaganda caused Fatah's popularity to soar. Arafat was quick to claim credit for bravely resisting and killing Israeli soldiers when, in fact, most of the fighting had been done by regular Jordanian troops who were then staunchly supporting the fedayeen.

In those days Hussein was faced with a *force majeur* and chose to ride the fedayeen bandwagon rather than be flattened by it. He said at a news conference after Karameh: "One could say we are all fedayeen," adding, "what can we be expected to do with regard to a people that has been driven from its home and has lost everything? Must we shoot them? Destroy them?"

Two years later, in Jordan's devastating civil war, Hussein ordered his tanks to move against the fedayeen and gave orders for artillery to shell Palestinian refugee camps.

In opposing the fedayeen, Hussein was acting to save his throne and ensure the continuation of the Hashemite dynasty, which derived from the Bedouin Arabs of the Saudi Arabian peninsula. Jordan had been created by the British in 1921 on territory originally considered part of Palestine. In imposing Hussein's grandfather, Abdullah, on the indigenous Palestinian population, the British were partially fulfilling a promise made to the Hashemite family in return for the participation of the desert Bedouin in the First World War on the side of the British against the Turks! Following the 1948 Arab-Israeli war, Abdullah annexed the West Bank of the Jordan which had been allocated by the United Nations to a proposed Palestinian Arab state.

After the Six-Day War, Fatah and the other guerrilla organizations established their principal bases on Jordanian territory and drew most of their members from among Palestinians living in Jordan. The Jordanian border allowed relatively easy access to the populated Arab areas captured by Israel in the War. Hussein thought fedayeen harassment would prevent any possibility of a prolonged

Israeli occupation of the West Bank and the regularization of Arab existence leading to the possible emergence of an autonomous entity. The King felt fedayeen incursions would prevent residents of the West Bank from settling into what he considered a dangerous mood of tranquillity. He was prepared to grant the fedayeen permission to operate against Israel, but only under Jordanian supervision and certainly not at the expense of his prestige and power.

Hussein soon realized that he could not support the guerrilla demands for total freedom of action within Jordan without relinquishing a portion of his country's political independence. Soon a fedayeen substate had emerged and the guerrillas boasted immunity to Hussein's laws and extra-territorial rights. The fedayeen regarded themselves as an army free of the established authority of the Jordanian army. Fatah and some of the other groups went about in their own uniforms and their vehicles bore fedayeen insignia and license plates. The fedayeen invited Jordanian youth subject to the draft to join them instead of the army and offered them three or four times the wages paid by the government forces.

The fedayeen created parallel civilian institutions of their own and refused to recognize the validity of Jordanian courts. They usurped the government's revenue-collecting privileges and collected taxes for themselves among sympathizers. Fedayeen set up roadblocks and closed off access to travelers lacking a permit issued by fedayeen authorities. Once Prince Hassan, Hussein's brother, was prevented from entering fedayeen headquarters in Karameh and on another occasion Hussein's wife, the English-born Munah, was stopped while riding in a royal convoy and kidnapped for several hours.

Hussein was also being humiliated by the presence of foreign Arab forces on his soil. An Iraqi division in northern Jordan, which had arrived on the eve of the Six-Day War, and units of the Saudi Arabian army, as well as Egyptian military personnel operating radar installations and anti-aircraft batteries in southern Jordan and Syrian artillery units made Hussein feel he was losing control. Syria and Egypt actively supported the fedayeen and reviled the king for attempting to regulate their activities.

Jordan's civilian population suffered because of the Jordanian army's collaboration with the fedayeen by providing cover-fire and making intelligence reports available. Israel retaliated by aerial strikes on fertile Jordan Valley. Extensive irrigation systems were destroyed and thousands of valley residents abandoned their homes to seek greater safety away from the border. Their places were taken by fedayeen units. In the town of Karameh alone, only 1000 persons out of an original population of 15,000 remained following the establishment of Fatah's command post there. The Jordanian army tried to prevent the large-scale evacuation of the valley, but despite roadblocks and checkpoints the villagers surged away from their homes, now jeopardized by the fedayeen.

Palestinian civilians were repeatedly exposed to fedayeen—Israeli crossfire, and Aqaba, Jordan's only seaport, was made vulnerable to Israeli reprisal when a gentlemen's agreement was broken and fedayeen shelled the Israeli Red Sea port of Eilat only a few miles away.

In the fall of 1968, the first clashes between Jordanian forces and fedayeen took place. Hussein limited anti-fedayeen action to a small group of guerrillas known as the "Victory Battalion," an offshoot of the Syrian Saiqah organization. After a series of small-scale confrontations a new agreement was signed between the government and the guerrillas. It was the first of many accords that would be broken.

The power of the fedayeen extremists grew from day

to day. George Habash, leader of the PFLP, began to openly question the necessity of Hussein's regime. Would it not be better, his followers argued, for the fedayeen to overthrow Hussein and replace him with a Palestinian regime? Habash and the extremists were in the minority in this respect as most fedayeen agreed with Yasir Arafat that in their present situation the best course for the fedayeen would be to continue their war against Israel and to refrain from attacking Arab governments, including Jordan. Behind Fatah's stance was the reluctance of most of the fedayeen groups to take responsibility for governing Jordan. Establishing a fedayeen-backed government in Jordan would serve to dispel the much-promoted notion of the homeless Palestinians.

Hussein tried various means of assuaging the guerrillas and sought to win their favor through political and rhetorical gestures. When appointing the government of Premier Bahajat Al Tahouni in August, 1969, Hussein attempted to make himself more acceptable to the guerrillas and his Palestinian subjects by emphasizing to Al Tahouni the need to find a military solution for the struggle with Israel. Hussein also hinted that he would accept the principle of self-determination for residents of the West Bank following Israeli withdrawal. Despite these overtures, tension continued in Jordan and in February, 1970, Hussein issued an order forbidding the fedayeen from carrying weapons within Amman. The resulting Palestinian demonstrations made the King retreat and the order was rescinded.

Fedayeen daring inside Jordan increased in direct proportion to their military failures against Israel. Among their demands was the removal of several members of Hussein's cabinet considered anti-fedayeen.

In June, 1970, rioting broke out following the attempt by several members of the PFLP to force Jordanian soldiers to contribute to the fedayeen. The guerrillas were jailed and protest riots were staged in Amman. The rampaging fedayeen seized hotels and held European guests as hostages, threatening to shoot them if Hussein did not release the imprisoned fedayeen or tried to use the army against them. Habash's men abducted and murdered the U.S. military attaché in Amman, raped several American women, and injured a French diplomat. The Jordanian army shelled a refugee camp in retaliation. The conflict finally came to an end with a joint declaration by Hussein and Arafat claiming agreement on outstanding issues but in reality signifying the King's capitulation to fedayeen pressure. Hussein yielded to the Palestinians' insistence on dictating who would serve in the government and what army commanders would be dismissed.

The truce deteriorated rapidly over the summer of 1970 and in September a new cycle of conflict began. Fedayeen ambushed Hussein's road escort and fired bazookas at the King's car. Hussein escaped uninjured, but several members of his party were hurt. The incident was the spark that ignited the civil war. The hijacking of three international jetliners by members of the PFLP further underscored the King's impotence and the frustrated army presented him with an ultimatum which gave Hussein no choice but to order his forces into action against the fedayeen who in the meantime had taken control of the northern city of Irbid and declared it the capital of the "liberated zone."

On September 17, Hussein's newly formed military government ordered the armored units, comprised mainly of Bedouin soldiers and U.S.-made tanks, against fedayeen strongholds, while other forces consisting of Palestinians, opened a fierce offensive on refugee camps where the guerrillas had installed themselves. Immense devastation and loss of civilian life resulted from the fighting as some 7000 armed fedayeen sought to turn back the well-equipped and disciplined Jordanian army, the best fighting force in the Arab world. In the ten-day civil war an estimated 2000 fedayeen were killed. The Palestinian guerrillas were incapable of successfully engaging in open warfare. In grim confrontations inside refugee camps, tough Bedouin soldiers systematically smashed the trigger fingers of fedayeen who desperately tried to hide among Palestinian women and children.

Despite their frequent promises, the 18,000-man Iraqi division stationed in Jordan with 200 Soviet-supplied tanks did not intervene on the side of the fedayeen. Syria, however, moved in a tank force disguised as a unit of the Palestine Liberation Army. The 285 Soviet-made Syrian tanks were pushed back across the border by Hussein's armor and jets. The involvement of the Syrians was a source of concern to the United States and Israel, who feared Hussein's overthrow and his replacement with a fedayeen regime friendly to Russia and Peking. Moscow had condoned the Syrian intervention and there were indications that the Russians had promised Damascus rear support in the event of an Israeli attack. The Soviet Union apparently was interested in probing America's readiness to defend her interests in the Mideast and possibly thought the Syrian invasion could serve as a test situation.

Had Hussein's forces failed to stop the Syrian tanks or had Iraq's division intervened, the United States and Israel would have taken coordinated military action. A plan worked out in Washington with Israeli diplomats envisioned an Israeli ground and air attack on the Syrian tanks, while the United States used the Sixth Fleet and air units to safeguard Israel's rear and flanks from Egyptian or Soviet attacks in the Suez Canal area.

The well-publicized Israeli troop build-up near the Jordanian border and the American military alerts, together with warnings conveyed to Moscow by Washington, persuaded the Soviet Union that it would be prudent to withdraw the Syrian tank force and discourage the Iraqis from fulfilling their promises to take the fedayeen's side.

By Wednesday, September 23, Syria apparently acting on the Kremlin's instructions, had withdrawn her battered tank force. With the Syrian threat ended, Hussein was clearly victorious in the bitter contest. But Amman was in shambles and thousands of non-fedayeen civilian Palestinians were dead and injured as a result of the Jordanian tank and artillery attacks on refugee centers where the fedayeen had positioned themselves. On September 25, Hussein and Arafat signed a new agreement at the urging of President Nasser of Egypt who died a few days later.

An Arab summit conference appointed a watchdog committee to enforce the accord and all parties, including King Hussein, signed a declaration promising unlimited support for "the Palestine revolution until its aims were realized: full liberation and the defeat of the oppressive Israeli enemy."

In early October, a secret meeting took place on the Israeli-Jordanian border between King Hussein and Deputy Premier Yigal Allon. Speaking in Arabic, the two embraced and exchanged compliments. Allon praised the King's courage and congratulated him on his victory. Hussein thanked Israel for concentrating troops on the border as a deterrent to the Syrians. The King was impressed with Israeli intelligence for always knowing where to attack fedayeen strongholds.

"Often we would wonder why you were bombing a certain area," Hussein confided to the Israeli leader. "But afterward we would find fedayeen tunnels and fortifications. I now can see what fantastic intelligence you have."

Allon appealed to the King to negotiate a separate settlement with Israel. "Now you have the opportunity to assume an honored position," Allon told him in the ornate Arabic style. "You have consolidated your rule and controlled the Syrians. Now you can settle our conflict."

Allon went on to describe his plan for the West Bank and the string of fortified settlements along the perimeter that would give Israel a military presence as insurance against renewed Palestinian terrorism. In return for this security belt, Allon offered Hussein a corridor to Gaza where he would have access to the Mediterranean, something landlocked Jordan had always desired. But Hussein replied he could never relinquish Arab land and the meeting ended cordially but inconclusively.

Hussein's plan for an East and West Bank Federation issued in the spring of 1972 provided for a semi-autonomous Palestinian state on the West Bank. Despite Israel's ostensible rejection, there were similarities between the Hussein plan and Allon's thinking.

A serious rift between Egypt and the fedayeen had developed as a result of President Nasser's acceptance of a United States peace initiative that called for a cease-fire in Suez and negotiations with Israel. Guerrilla leaders spoke out against the Egyptian action and pledged undying resistance to any agreement that would recognize Israel's national existence and regularize Mideast borders. Nasser responded by closing down Fatah's radio station in Cairo and warning the fedayeen through articles in the press that they alone could not bring about a solution to the Mideast problems and were expendable.

The loss of Nasser's support resulted in the cutting off of funds made available to the fedayeen by the Arab-League nations. In 1971, the Arab League did not pay its yearly allocation to the Palestine Liberation Organization and Saudi Arabia canceled her annual fedayeen subsidy, which had amounted to more than a million dollars. King Faisal was reportedly displeased because of the corruption and the influence of the left-wing groups, even within the ideologically conservative Fatah. Faisal was said to doubt the future of the fedayeen in view of their setbacks in Jordan. Egyptian, Iraqi, and Syrian allocations to the Palestinian Liberation Forces also ceased.

Money troubles, strained relations with Arab governments, and diminished prestige aggravated the internal differences on tactics and ideology that rent the fedayeen movement. Under attack as an ineffectual leader, more concerned with publicity and bourgeois comforts than the struggle against Israel, Yasir Arafat tried to rid Fatah of a growing reputation for indulgence. He closed all but one of the movement's offices in Lebanon and declared a new policy of self-criticism and a return to secret operations. Several fedayeen conferences aimed at achieving solidarity failed and the structure of the P.L.O. splintered. The President of Egypt concentrated on consolidating his regime, and the world's attention was diverted by abortive diplomatic efforts to bring the Jews and Arabs together.

Having lost the general support of the Nasserist masses in Arab lands and having antagonized the army and much of the population in Jordan, the fedayeen were an easy target for Hussein who had decided to rid his nation of the Palestinian guerrilla "state within a state." The Jordanian army, beefed up with an estimated $30 million worth of U.S. military aid, pressed its offensive during the winter months of 1971. By April the guerrillas had been driven out of Amman and the key towns of Jarash and Irbid. In the beginning of summer, more than

2000 fedayeen were bottled up in the hills between Ajlun and Jarash in northwest Jordan.

Hussein and his anti-fedayeen premier, Wasfi Tal, launched the final showdown in July as the Jordanian army surrounded the guerrilla encampments. This time Syria avoided involvement and other Arab countries offered little more than statements in defense of the fedayeen. Jordanian artillery began shelling on July 12 and between the 13th and the 15th tank and infantry units closed in, rounding up some 2000 guerrillas and killing approximately 700. Some 100 fedayeen fled across the Jordan River to Israel where they surrendered. One fedayeen said bitterly, "Better to die by Israeli hands than to be killed by an Arab brother."

In Israel the guerrillas were interrogated and many of them who had been active in Fatah renounced the fedayeen but said they still wanted to "liberate the homeland." They said they had decided to cross over to Israel rather than Syria because they feared they would be tortured in Syrian jails. About forty of the fedayeen who had not taken part in the actions against Israel and the remaining sixty were imprisoned.

Once the captured fedayeen in Jordan had been disarmed and dispersed only about 500 chose to remain in Jordan where they swore loyalty to the King. The remainder either returned to their homes in Jordan, Syria, and other Arab countries, or joined fedayeen groups in Lebanon and Syria. Defying Arab criticism, Hussein had crushed the fedayeen and saved his throne.

At the end of November, the fedayeen avenged themselves on Wasfi Tal when a group calling itself "The Black Hand of September" (named for the September, 1970, civil war) gunned down the Jordanian Premier and Defense Minister in the lobby of the Sheraton Hotel in Cairo where he was heading Jordan's delegation to the Arab League Council meeting on military strategy against Israel. Tal was replaced by Ahmed Lozi, another hardliner who was told by Hussein that "the policy established under Wasfi Tal is to be the same policy of your administration."

With the fedayeen threat ended in Jordan, attention shifted to Lebanon where a clash between Lebanese police and fedayeen in early 1972 reminded observers of the renewed potential for Palestinian agitation in Lebanon, where internally things had been quiet since the battling between guerrillas and the Lebanese troops in 1969. In January, 1972, new concentrations of fedayeen in bases near Lebanese villages attacked northern Israeli settlements with artillery and katyusha rockets. Israel struck six miles inside Lebanese territory and killed an unknown number of guerrillas, several houses were also blown up. Israeli intelligence said trainers and advisers from Libya were with the fedayeen.

Since before the Six-Day War Lebanon had been an important center of Palestinian political activity. The camps containing 75,000 refugees were natural recruiting grounds for the fedayeen and the relatively unbridled press of Beirut made that city the center of fedayeen propaganda and fund-raising among Arab banks and business enterprises.

The Lebanese government was tolerant of Palestinian activity as long as it was confined to sloganeering and fund-raising. Lebanon wanted to remain unentangled in the Arab-Israeli dispute and was the only one of Israel's neighbors to avoid the Six-Day War. As a democratic pro-Western island in the Arab world, Lebanon was a nonbelligerent dedicated to the preservation of the delicate constitutional arrangement that carefully divided offices and power between Christians and Moslems. With Syria's active encouragement, the fedayeen in 1969 attempted to diminish the influence of the Maronite Christians and hasten a takeover of the pro-fedayeen Sunni Moslems.

Syria's involvement in the internal affairs of Lebanon derived from her traditional rejection of a separate and independent Lebanon. Syria and Lebanon had been part of the Ottoman Empire until the end of World War I, and Damascus had always thought of Lebanon as rightfully belonging to Greater Syria. Syria resented the protection of France enjoyed by Christian-dominated Lebanon and was jealous of Lebanon's economic prosperity. No matter what regime ruled in Damascus one objective remained the same: the establishment of a Greater Syria that would annex Lebanon. As one means of pursuing this aim Syria encouraged large-scale fedayeen infiltration from both Syria and Jordan into Lebanon. In 1968 fedayeen took up positions along the southwestern slopes of Mt. Hermon, near the post-1967 border with Israel. Beirut responded cautiously to this intrusion, hoping the guerrillas would not cause disturbances.

While all of the 150,000 Palestinians in Lebanon were in favor of the fedayeen, as were many of Lebanon's Moslems, the Christians objected to the growing number of armed guerrillas and insisted on maintaining Lebanon's neutrality. It was feared that fedayeen activity would provoke Israeli retaliation. Soon fedayeen attacks on Israel, launched from bases in the border region the international press was calling "Fatahland" shook Lebanon's political stability. Pro-Nasserists, pro-Baathists, and Communists united in pressing for total fedayeen freedom of action. Every attempt by the government to reach a modus vivendi with the guerrillas failed, and two premiers were forced to resign, one in 1968 and the other in 1969.

The army, most of whose officers were Christian, was opposed to the fedayeen infiltration. While much of the army supported the Palestinian cause, it was against the introduction of alien armed forces into the country and feared the situation would give Israel a pretext for invading and occupying the southern portion of the country, where the government had been powerless to prevent the Fatah and Saiqah buildup.

The refusal of the fedayeen to heed government appeals for a cessation of raids launched from Lebanese territory led to clashes between army and guerrilla forces in March and April of 1969. Units of the Syrian-backed Saiqah had been steadily infiltrating the country and constituted a Trojan horse serving the Baathist ambition of subverting Lebanon. Saiqah units extended their presence beyond "Fatahland" to other areas of southern Lebanon and were forcibly resisted by Lebanese army and police. A new government headed by a Maronite Christian military man and supported by rightist Christian leaders roused public opinion against the fedayeen and at least half the population opposed the guerrillas.[1]

Syria and Iraq exploited the confusion and unrest in Lebanon by openly appealing to the Moslem population to oppose the government and support the fedayeen. Nasser publicly took the fedayeen's part by declaring that no Arab nation would be able to stay out of the sphere of Palestinian guerrilla action. The pressure brought to bear on Lebanon by other Arab nations mounted and effectively deterred the Lebanese from acting firmly against the fedayeen. By the end of May, 1969, a temporary truce had been negotiated between Yasir Arafat and the Lebanese army under Cairo's auspices.

The uneasy cease-fire held through the summer, but in October fighting flared again in and around refugee camps that were fedayeen strongholds. Palestinian demands were stepped up and now included a provision for establishing a separate fedayeen army in Lebanon. Pro-Palestinian riots in Tripoli and demonstrations in Beirut were quelled by Lebanese troops and Syria introduced an armored column of troops disguised as fedayeen fighters. Under the leadership of Syria and Egypt the Arab states lined up in condemning Lebanon and denouncing the army which refused to stand by idly as the fedayeen moved further and further toward imperiling the nation by provoking Israeli reprisals, which would inevitably increase in severity.

In October, 1969, fedayeen, assisted by Syrian army units, attacked Lebanese police posts along the Syrian-Lebanese border. The Lebanese border troops surrounded refugee camps and drove fedayeen away from the western border of Israel back to Fatahland around Mt. Hermon. To the north a critical battle took place to determine control over the road from Fatahland to Syria, a major supply route for the fedayeen. Despite full Syrian artillery support, the fedayeen were unable to cope with the Lebanese troops who deeply resented the Palestinians for upsetting Lebanon's peaceful status quo.

The fighting lasted more than a month and ended with a pact signed in Cairo between the guerrillas and the army. The new accord allowed the fedayeen to operate from Lebanese territory but under strict limitations. They were forbidden to fire on Israel from Lebanon, were ordered not to establish bases near villages that would then be vulnerable to Israeli retaliation, and were told to stop training at refugee camps. The agreement reaffirmed Lebanon's sovereignty over the refugee camps but control stayed in the hands of the guerrillas who were authorized to set up local committees to deal with problems of hygiene, lodging, and administration. Nasser feared a premature takeover by the fedayeen in Lebanon and had tailored the pact accordingly. Syria regretted that once again it had missed an opportunity to successfully foment anarchy in neighboring Lebanon. Damascus was warned indirectly by Israel that any further attempt to invade Lebanon or precipitate civil war in that country would be met by Israeli action to protect her border and that this might entail the seizure of Lebanese territory to preserve "regional tranquillity."

Israel was disturbed by the fedayeen concentrations in Lebanon because the border between the two countries was the easiest one for guerrilla warfare due to the lack of natural boundaries. The fedayeen were repeatedly shelling Israeli towns and settlements near the border and reprisals had no effect. What for years had been a quiet, inhabited border underwent a transformation similar to what had happened in Jordan. Farming villages became ghost towns, victims of fedayeen infiltration. Failing to gain desired results with short-range, limited retaliatory penetrations, Israel planned a more ambitious operation against Fatahland.

On May 20, 1970, an Israeli school bus carrying children from rural settlements to a regional school was ambushed with bazookas by a fedayeen group. Twelve were killed, including two teachers, and other children were severely injured and maimed for life. The provocation shocked the Israelis and set the mood for a dramatic, daylong sweep into Fatahland that cleaned up nests of guerrillas, and established Israel's presence as policeman in the hilly Lebanese border region. Israel subsequently paved roads and took up fortified positions at elevated observation points. The fedayeen were pushed out of much of Fatahland and the villagers returned. A security belt, a few miles in width, was established along the border and quiet has now been restored at least until the reappearance of fedayeen following their expulsion from Jordan. The fedayeen in Lebanon were well back from the border for a time and found it extremely difficult to cross over to the Israeli side where patrols and Druze scouts keep every foot of the border under surveillance. Many of the Lebanese border villagers actively cooperated in keeping the peace by refusing any assistance to the fedayeen, who are generally regarded in that areas as an unwelcome foreign element. The guerrillas, however, intensified shelling and rocket firing and damaged Israeli settlements.

The fedayeen in Lebanon as of the beginning of 1972 were ready once again to heat up the conflict with Israel and seemed to be playing out a familiar scenario in their relations with the Lebanese government and that nation's 15,000-man army. Israel warned that continued fedayeen harassment would provoke major military action.

The diplomatic impasse in the Middle East threatened to give way to renewed Egyptian-Israeli fighting and the guerrillas were undoubtedly encouraged by the failure of the peace effort. Fear of Israeli retaliation and deep penetrations into southern Lebanon would again draw the Beirut government into conflict with the guerrillas. As long as a substantial fedayeen presence remains in Lebanon and Syria, with Soviet arms and other support—and the Soviet continues its patronage against both Israel and Lebanon's fragile Christian-Moslem balance—there is a real danger of large-scale warfare.

Premier Saeb Salam of Lebanon noted the deteriorating situation and following Israeli reprisals in January, 1972, insisted that the guerrillas move their bases and offices from border villages to uninhabited areas, which would be less vulnerable to Israeli retaliation. An indication of Salam's success was a report at the end of January that Yasir Arafat had established new Fatah headquarters in the Dera region of Syria, near the Jordanian border.

Increased fedayeen activity originating in Syria elicited an Israeli air strike toward the end of January, the first aerial attack on Syria in nineteen months. Fedayeen concentrations around Dera were bombed in reprisal for several fedayeen actions, including the decapitating of an Israeli engineer in the Golan Heights by a band of guerrillas.

Syria's armed forces are equipped and trained by the Soviet Union and in the beginning of 1972 there were signs that Moscow had decided to extend this type of military support more openly to the fedayeen under Syria's control. Arms would still be supplied through the Syrians, but reports originating from Western intelligence sources said the Russians had promised Arafat field hospital equipment and medical assistance for fedayeen wounded in action against Israel. This was a strong hint that Russia had embarked on a policy of endorsing attacks on Israel despite the dangers of reprisals. This development could be traced to Communist China's championship in the United Nations of the Palestinians, and Peking's well-publicized policy of training and arming fedayeen groups, particularly the Maoist Popular Front for the Liberation of Palestine.

Moscow and Peking, competing with each other for popularity among the fedayeen, could spark stepped-up campaigns against Israel and encourage the inexorable cycle of terror-reprisal that at least once before had precipitated all-out war.

The fedayeen have failed so far in their war against Israel and their struggle to reform reactionary Arab regimes. And they have not been able to accomplish their dreams of changing the traditionally inequitable social structure of Arab life. Despite considerable propaganda concerning the creation of a new Arab fighting man, it is clear that the privileges of class and family, the heritage of the past, haunts the Palestinian revolution.

Research carried out among thousands of fedayeen prisoners by Israeli investigators has uncovered the fact that few of their officers, who are generally from upper-class families, participate in actual combat. Consequently, officer casualties are extremely light and the rank-and-file fedayeen bear the brunt of exceedingly heavy casualty rates. The protected position of officers is the bane of most Arab armies and the fedayeen have introduced no basic change in the extensive privileges granted the upper-class, educated Arab.

General Rehaveam Zeevi, the Israeli officer in charge of patrols in the Jordan Valley, comments: "The fedayeen officers, even the junior ones, do not go into action. The bands captured in the Jordan Valley do not comprise the Fatah advocates one used to see at universities in Europe and the United States. The propagandists, those that yell about 'freeing their usurped lands,' are not the ones risking their lives to penetrate Israeli territory. The example of an officer who calls out 'follow me' to his men does not exist among the fedayeen."

Israeli investigators have also come to the conclusion that monetary incentives are as important, if not more so, to fedayeen recruits as ideological and nationalistic sentiments. It was found that among Jordanian youth the higher pay offered by Fatah, approximately $54 a month, and the privilege of carrying a gun at all times were far stronger incentives than the low pay of the Jordanian army, about $13.40 a month, and the more conventional discipline.

Before the Six-Day War, the effectiveness of the fedayeen was close to zero, even though some members of

Fatah sent into Israel had had experience in sabotage. After the June war a gradual improvement in fedayeen operational ability was noted. Advanced training at army bases in Egypt and Syria and sometimes in Communist China for a select few enabled the guerrillas to cause death and destruction among Israeli and Arab civilians, but did not help turn the tide in military confrontations with Israel.

The failure of the fedayeen to establish a functional underground in the occupied areas is perhaps the most disappointing defeat the Palestine Liberation Movement has had to justify in view of its emphasis of popular resistance to Israeli occupation as the first step in the eventual people's war against the Zionist enemy. The disproportionate number of Arab deaths and casualties as a result of fedayeen actions demonstrates the lack of success Palestinian guerrillas have had in winning support among Arabs living under Israeli administrations.

The fedayeen tend to blame Israeli intelligence for many of their setbacks. And although Israel will not confirm it, there is no doubt that Israeli agents have often infiltrated fedayeen cells and broken up terrorist conspiracies while still in the process of organizing. The thousands of fedayeen in Israeli jails and their readiness to cooperate with their interrogators, a willingness uncharacteristic of dedicated resistance fighters, is an important factor in Israeli undercover work. The imprisoned fedayeen show little inclination to return to the struggle. The apathy that has afflicted Arab society for so long is also evident among the fedayeen, who once removed from the exhortations of their leaders and the adulation of the press and radio, fall into a pitiful state of disillusionment and bewilderment.

The fedayeen have so far been unable to frighten

Israel into a premature withdrawal from occupied territory or the abandonment of sovereignty over the Jewish part of the land called Palestine. The only accomplishment of fedayeen terrorism has been to harden Israeli thinking on the subject of a possible rapprochement with the Palestinians. Since 1880, Arab terrorists and guerrilla war has accompanied Jewish settlement in Palestine, but it is not a phenomenon likely to cause a basic change in the commitment of Jews to Israel and their determination to defend their state.

If the Middle East is ever to know peace there will have to be a settlement between Israel and the Palestinians. The deeds and propaganda of the fedayeen have underscored this truth and emphasized the basic dilemma of two peoples in conflict over the same land. Perhaps some day there will be understanding between the Palestinian people and Israel, but the history of the Middle East does not nourish hope or sustain illusion. The state of Jewish and Arab relations today offers little more than bloodshed in the future. The fedayeen can never hope to regain Palestine by destroying Israel. They can only continue to harass and to kill. Many of their victims will be Jews, but even more will be Arabs.

NOTE

1. Survey conducted by the Beirut newspaper *Al Nahar* showed that more than 50 percent of the Lebanese people opposed the fedayeen in 1969.

Index